When an elder statesman decides to share his thoughts with us, and there is no preferment left for him other than to face his maker, we should listen carefully. The Truth Will Set You Free *is the insight of a man with vast knowledge and experience of human frailty and his words of wisdom deserve a wide audience not just for its scholarship, but its human understanding. This is a book for the old and the young alike. In fact, I wish I'd read it when I was eighteen.*

Lord Archer of Weston-super-Mare, writer

I highly recommend that everyone interested in helping us build a better world read this wise and timely book. All Christians face unprecedented challenges in our complicated world today, and Lord Carey's reflections can help us address them.

James A. Baker III, 61st US Secretary of State

*When George Carey retired as Archbishop of Canterbury in 2002, he wrote his memoirs (*Know the Truth*). But writing did not stop him ministering, travelling, reflecting and engaging; and now in his eighties he writes up an astonishing range of enterprises he has pursued. Some have roots in his time as Archbishop, some are new in his retirement. Told thematically, rather than chronologically, they include the World Economic Forum, vigorous initiatives towards other faiths, picketing the World Bank re. needs of suffering countries, and visiting Rwanda and Myanmar, to name but a few. He has entered into church conflicts, not only in the USA, but also with a chapter on the demeaning of George Bell in this country, and, sadly, another telling the story of how his own retirement ministry has been marred by the Peter Ball affair. As I expected, he finishes with a burst of how* *he has won through these many challenges, strong in a much tried, but well-matured, faith. You can hear George Carey, a good friend of mine, speaking.*

Colin Buchanan, former Bishop of Woolwich,
author of *Historical Dictionary of Anglicanism*

This is such a deeply moving and inspirational book that I could hardly put it down!

It describes in moving detail the amazing life of George Carey from his boyhood in London's East End, leaving school without any GCSEs, through a fascinating range of responsibilities and positions to become Archbishop of Canterbury.

George writes with humility, describing in great detail the many challenges he has surmounted, together with his wife Eileen.

He has the courage to put on record some of the conflicts he has encountered, especially the profoundly turbulent time when he was dismissed from practising as an Anglican priest.

But throughout the book there are inspirational descriptions of people and situations bringing great personal support and professional endorsement.

Overall, the lasting blessings of this book are the stories of his courage to fulfil God's calling and his unfailing faith which maintains light for himself and others in many dark situations – providing personal evidence of how "The Truth Can Set You Free".

Baroness Cox, Founder and CEO of Hart

This is a book of two parts: inspiring memoirs covering life after Canterbury and a shocking indictment of incompetence and vexatious decision making at the highest levels of the Church of England. Lord Carey's side of the saga has remained unheard for too long.

Lord Griffiths of Fforestfach, former Chair of Policy Unit in Margaret Thatcher's cabinet

In this enthralling book, service and compassion for the poor are central themes. This is as true for Shintoism as it is for Christianity. Both faiths want to make a difference. I applaud Lord Carey's remarkable work, and thank him for the support he has given to my philanthropic activity in Cambodia and elsewhere.

Dr Haruhisa Handa, philanthropist, Shinto priest, artist and entrepreneur

As Lord George Carey points out in this poignant and timely work, "There can be no true renewal of faith … unless clergy remain rooted in the faith and by its mission." For over half a century, Lord Carey has served faithfully our Lord and the children of God as a compassionate and courageous leader who at all times and in all seasons has been, and continues to be, rooted in the historic faith and mission of Christ. This book could not be more timely as the world emerges from a long season of darkness. People are hungry for meaning and purpose – they are hungry for truth! As many Christian leaders have said over the centuries, a long faithful obedience in the same direction is an absolutely essential quality in a life of discipleship. In a humble, yet honestly frank, personal testimony, this incredible work reminds us of the debt the Church, and the world, owe to our 103rd Archbishop of Canterbury

– a friend to all he meets, and a living witness to the enduring power of truth! May our faith be renewed yet again by these marvellous words!

> The Reverend Dr Russell Jones Levenson, Jr, OStJ, Rector, St. Martin's Episcopal Church Sub-Prelate, US Priory of the Order of St John of Jerusalem

In this deeply reflective and personal narrative about his life journey, Lord Carey highlights his laser focus on the world's poor and vulnerable communities. He links his deep faith to the many practical ways that religious communities do and can address suffering and, more important still, paths to more fulfilling lives. That is the mission of the World Faiths Development Dialogue that he co-founded with World Bank President James D. Wolfensohn: spirit and hands need to work together with a clear sense of purpose.

> Professor Katherine Marshall, CEO of WFDD, former assistant of Jim Wolfensohn

Written with striking honesty, this book sets out the values which inspired his ministry before and after becoming Archbishop of Canterbury. Humbly admitting mistakes, he also describes the pain unjustly inflicted on him and his family – not least on his son the Rev Mark Carey. Sharing George's ideals for greater justice and peace in our world, better leadership, and so much else besides, I know that he respects my differing view on physician-assisted dying.

> Gerald O'Collins, SJ, AC, Jesuit Theological College, Parkville, Australia, former Professor of Systematic and Fundamental Theology, the Pontifical Gregorian University, Rome

It was a pleasure to invite Lord Carey to join the Foundation Board of the World Economic Forum. His presence and contribution was a reminder that issues of faith, integrity, leadership and development are common to us all. Lord Carey's book is an honest reflection on a long career that deserves a wide audience.

Prof Klaus Schwab, Founder and Executive
Chairman of the World Economic Forum

I was raised up in a Ugandan village, Masooli, blessed with the good soil for growing maize. Our elders, especially of the East African Revival, encouraged us to see the breaking horizon of Hope. Archbishop George Carey, who ordained me Bishop in the Church of God in 1996, in his second autobiography, has done just that. The Truth Will Set You Free *opens for us Archbishop George encountering God's bounty and unmerited favour. The fruit was made visible in the Decade of Evangelism: the time of our life for young people. George's strong foundations of Scripture and the work of the Holy Spirit gave him permission to enter uncharted waters of what it means to be an ambassador of heaven. His second autobiography is a must read for all who wish to explore mission and evangelism and walk closely with God in Christ.*

Baron Sentamu of Lindisfarne in
Northumberland and Masooli in the Republic
of Uganda, former Archbishop of York

THE TRUTH WILL
SET YOU FREE

THE TRUTH WILL
SET YOU FREE

GEORGE CAREY

ISAAC PUBLISHING

CONTENTS

Foreword

"Life is a gift of God; but a gift not to be owned as an ornament or an award or as an honorary title, but to be lived as a vocation, with a purpose, a sense of meaning and mission." So said the Armenian Catholicos, Karekin I (1932-99). The Catholicos's attitude is shared by George Carey, the 103rd Archbishop of Canterbury, who saw his whole life as a ministry and a mission. At the point of retirement, when most would opt for an easier life, he chose to become a leader on the global stage, and the life of this "man with a mission" unfolded in a remarkable way. Some might say he had been guided by circumstances, but he himself would say he was guided by God. His wife Eileen continued to be his strength and support in this new phase of his work and ministry, a constant encouragement and dignified presence.

The priest, the bishop and the archbishop was already a theologian and academic. After retirement – the period on which this book concentrates – he went on to enter the world of economics and politics, becoming a negotiator and a legislator. He joined the eclectic Foundation Board of the World Economic Forum, which meets annually in Davos, his role being Co-ordinator of faith leaders. Engagement with religious communities was one of the many and diverse objectives of this most significant gathering, which aims at both private and public cooperation.

The 9/11 attacks on the USA had taken place barely a year before his retirement and, in the massive global upheaval that followed, Lord Carey was active in working to develop relationships with the House of Islam and seeking to find a way forward. The reputation of not only Islam but all religions had taken a severe battering because of 9/11. After discussion with Professor Klaus Schwab, founder of the World Economic Forum, Lord Carey took on the responsibility of working with Prince Turki bin Faisal al Saud to create the "Council of 100", meaning a hundred leaders from religion, politics, business, art and journalism who were tasked with trying to bridge the divide between Islam and the West.

I first had the privilege of meeting Lord Carey many years ago at Lambeth Palace. He always had a great concern for the persecuted Church and this meeting was about the persecution of Christians in South Sudan. Naturally he does not remember our brief conversation in the midst of a busy conference, although his words have remained with me. Perhaps rather impertinently, I asked him about his priorities as archbishop but he answered me with typical gentle graciousness. He told me that, in his capacity as Archbishop of Canterbury, he saw his first responsibility as being to the Church of England, his second to the whole nation irrespective of their faith or beliefs, and his third to the Anglican Communion worldwide. It could be said that a fourth responsibility – to the world, to reshape it in terms of ethics and truth – has now come to the fore in his life.

Lord Carey is a person with the rare gift of moving freely in any milieu. From an Essex council estate, to the Principal's office at a theological college, to Lambeth Palace as archbishop with frequent interaction with the Royal Family, and finally to the House of Lords, he retained the ability to interact with people from all walks of life. The phrase *primus inter pares* most aptly applies to him. Whether conversing with leadership of the highest order or with "the man or woman in the street", he is always the same and can cross these boundaries in a way that very few can do. He has maintained his integrity and his transparency throughout.

A theme undergirding *The Truth Will Set You Free* is that of leadership in the modern world, and the personal qualities which good leadership requires. Compassion, care and love are qualities that Lord Carey admires in other leaders and also shows in his own life. He recounts a story of Nelson Mandela who, while attending the World Economic Forum, glanced at his watch and then asked if he could borrow someone's phone. Returning the phone after a brief call, he explained that, following his release from twenty-seven years in prison, he had promised his family that he would phone one of them every day at a certain time to express his love for them.

Lord Carey's own leadership is characterised not only by compassion and mercy but also by an enduring focus on justice, truth and righteousness. It is from this standpoint that he has examined the great issues of ethics and of how society should function.

Self-effacing and humble by nature, he is one who has had "greatness thrust upon him" yet has retained his remarkable and inspiring modesty. He is always seeking to learn from others. Of his time at Trinity College Bristol, where, as Principal, he had to rescue an institution with much potential but which was at the time in deep trouble, he writes:

> Leadership is rarely about dominating; it is essentially about keeping one's eye on the goal and encouraging others to share in the vision. I have often called leadership "the art of making things possible". It does not matter who gets the credit – so often the obstacle that gets in the way of growth – but that we achieve together what we most desire.

In his latter years, this most generous-hearted and meek of men has been presented with almost insurmountable problems. In *The Truth Will Set You Free*, he tells the story – without anger or rancour. The two decades of his retirement have been a time of enormous change and upheaval as society and Church wrestled with issues of sexuality and sexual abuse. In these turbulent debates, Lord Carey has stayed constant in terms of his faith and also in terms of his courtesy and self-restraint even when his own name was being dragged through the mud. From being, as Archbishop of Canterbury, the highest-ranking non-royal person in the country, he found himself in a position where he was forbidden to perform even the most basic duties of a priest when his "Permission to Officiate" was taken away from him (but later restored). He had to endure a prolonged barrage of criticism and undeserved animosity, but faced this with courage, equanimity and patience, supported and upheld as ever by Eileen, who willingly shared his pain, "disgrace" and humiliation. None of us can choose which challenges will come our way but we can choose how to respond to them: Lord Carey is a fine model for us to follow.

At the heart of everything is his deep spirituality, with Christ at the very centre of it. He has remained unwavering in his Christian faith and his view of Christ. He has retained also his Christ-like humility and his desire to seize every God-given opportunity for service. He exemplifies the words of the Lord Jesus (Matthew 23:11): "The greatest among you will be your servant."

Cor Episcopos Professor Patrick Sookhdeo PhD, DD
International Director of Barnabas Fund

July 2021

Introduction

It was never my intention to write a sequel to my autobiography *Know the Truth* which appeared shortly after I retired in 2002. The reason I am doing so now, nearly twenty years after retirement, is because of encouragement from many friends in recent years. One African bishop put it: "You have touched many lives and met so many leaders, please take up your pen." The clinching reason was when my friend, Patrick Sookhdeo, encouraged me to write and offered the publishing services of Barnabas Fund to do so. As I discussed this with Eileen and my family I could see many reasons for writing for the very last time, and it has to do with sharing experiences and thoughts with younger clergy and lay people.

Few will deny the unusual journey I have had: the first Archbishop to come from a solid working-class family and the first not to have the privilege of an Oxbridge education. However, that in itself is not all that important. What is more significant is that, since retirement, I have had almost a second career away from the Church and yet, in a curious way, representing it. Since retirement I have served on the Board of the World Economic Forum and brushed shoulders with the most powerful of leaders. I have presided over one of the largest Academy chains in the UK; co-founded a development charity with the President of the World Bank; served with Dr Handa, a Shinto priest, one of the most compassionate religious leaders in Asia; and have been and still am a crossbencher in the House of Lords.

Running as a thread through this book is the issue of leadership – in the business world as well as the Church. I have seen at very close hand some of the greatest figures in business life and I have been very impressed. My nearly ten years with the World Economic Forum brought me into close contact with top-class, intelligent people who believed in their work and gave their entire lives to it. I found myself asking: "What can these people teach us all about the character of leading and serving others? What moral instincts guide them; what insights may we draw from their work that might assist voluntary organisations like the Church?"

It goes almost without saying that, here and there, some will disagree with my observations. Towards the end of this book I mention three areas where serious disagreements exist between the current leadership of the Church of England and myself. This is very regrettable and it is on public record. I have felt it necessary to go into considerable detail because my side of the story has not been told. Obviously I am deeply sorry that this is necessary, but truth matters. Having said that, I bear no malice towards anyone and hope that, in general, my opinions will help forward the mission of a Church I have loved and given most of my life to. My intention is to help the Church, to assist future ministers as I reflect upon a rich and fulfilled ministry. I have good news to share as well as concerns about an institution I love. Anyone who has served the Church for as long, and in so many diverse ways as I have, will have few doubts that its ultimate future is secure. It has done and is doing a faithful work through its army of workers and through the ministry of thousands of parish churches. Do not, please, underestimate the sacramental presence and ministry of those glorious buildings built and maintained by love.

This volume is called *The Truth Will Set You Free* and continues the quotation from John's Gospel (8:32) that inspired the first part of my autobiography. My story is a clear answer to the question: "What difference does the Christian faith make?" In my case it freed me, changed me and gave me a purpose in life and a reason to exist. I cannot but be grateful. How can I have any regrets about the way my life has developed since my birth in the East End of London and early life in Dagenham? It was Thomas Traherne who declared that the entire business of religion is bounty on God's part and gratitude on ours – and that sums up my estimate of my life.

In writing this there are so many people who have touched my and Eileen's lives with grace and kindness. There are those who have gone ahead: our parents with their examples of unswerving love lived at the toughest of times. Then there have been those who have influenced us greatly: Rev E.P.C. Patterson, Rev Eric Vevers, Stephen Houghton, Peter and Phyllis Johnston, Liz Salmon, Michael and Rosemary Green,

Colin Buchanan, Roger Symon and Patrick Sookhdeo. There are those who have commented on chapters of this book and helped to make it more accurate or more readable: Katherine Marshall, Jonathan Romain, Andrew Chandler, Ruth Hildenbrandt Grayson, Kathy August and especially Rachel, Mark and Andrew Carey. Andrew in particular has been of great help in the writing of this book. Indeed, all of our wonderful children have been a huge blessing on our journey, with their partners: Rachel and Andy, Mark and Penny, Andrew and Helen, Lizzie and Steve.

They will be in no doubt that the outstanding person in my life is the woman I married sixty years ago. I met Eileen when she was a girl of seventeen and I had just been demobbed from the Royal Air Force. She has been the rock in my life and my true north; always there and unswervingly loyal, yet always herself.

Some years ago when staying at the home of the President of Sewanee University, Tennessee, I came across the words of Pete Seeger. Last year was the Diamond Anniversary of our marriage, and the words evoke the happiness we have shared together:

> "Over the hills I went one day
> Dreaming of myself and you
> And the springtime of years since first we met
> And all that we've been through.
> May I not with delight still dream
> Of the years of the summer and fall to be
> And the many, many verses still to be sung
> In the ballad of you and me."

Our marriage of sixty years and my ministry of nearly the same length have witnessed the most seismic of changes in the world and Church. It is to this that I now turn.

George Carey

1

Looking Back

*Twenty years from now you will be more disappointed
by the things you didn't do than by the ones you did.
So throw off the bowlines, sail away from the safe
harbour, catch the trade winds in your sails. Explore.
Dream. Discover.*

Mark Twain

Looking back is not encouraged in the Bible. Isaiah (43:18) urges:
"Do not remember the former things, neither consider the things
of old." St Paul likewise, that busy and diligent missionary, wrote to
the congregation of Philippi: "This one thing I do, forgetting those
things that are behind and reaching forth unto those things that are
before." (Philippians 3:13)

And it is true that one cannot dwell on the past. It is over and, if
one lingers on it too much, nostalgia and regret will easily take up
lodging in one's life and memory.

There is, of course, a proper place for remembering and it has to
do with thanksgiving and learning. This has been my experience
because I have much to be thankful for, as I look back at a long life
with all its twists and turns, hopes and disillusionment, fulfilment and

disappointment. This used to be called the doctrine of Providence which seems to have been dropped from much preaching today. But the doctrine is certainly there in such biblical verses as Romans 8:28: "All things work together for good for those who love God." Providence is confirmed by faithful living and service. The Lord is and remains faithful.

My Christian life was shaped by the Second World War. I was the eldest of five children born to our devoted parents: George, Dennis, the twins Robert and Ruby and Valerie. As children of working-class parents, the war was a frightening reality revealing the thinness of civilisation. We were evacuated three times when the war was most intense. We were reminded this was not a childhood game when we were rushed with our gas masks to the air raid shelter at the bottom of the garden. It was a matter of life and death. We did not need Winston Churchill's measured and serious tones coming from the wireless to inform us Britain was fighting for its survival. Indeed, the devastation caused by the evils of totalitarianism in both Germany and Russia nearly brought Western civilisation to its knees.

Paul Tillich's immensely powerful book *The Shaking of the Foundations*[1] sums up his feeling after the Second World War. One of the great theologians of the twentieth century, he was shaken to the core by the brutality and impact of that war. He had witnessed and experienced the evils of Nazi ideology. It was a war that ultimately led to the deaths of some seventy million people – six million of them Jews murdered in a country regarded at the time as the most civilised and educated nation of all. What was there left to believe in?

I was ten when that war ended. I was deeply shaken myself by the experience of seeing dogfights in the air over London, and by three evacuations to the countryside when the bombings were at their height. As peace came to the Western world nothing would ever be the same again – and to some extent this was good. It was a time to rebuild and look forward. Churchill, the warrior, was replaced by Attlee, the builder. From the brokenness of a ruined Britain a dynamic new world arose; the National Health Service was created, soldiers became civilians, houses were rebuilt and hope replaced fear.

Where was the Church in this child's mind? We did not go to church, but our lovely and dear parents were believers, and their faith in a loving and caring Creator underpinned their lives. Mind you, this inchoate faith did not impinge on the everyday events of our family much, but we instinctively shared a spirituality in common with much of the rest of the community. As I entered my teens I became aware that the Church was present in society as a powerful institution, through vicars, bishops and archbishops. But it was all remote from ordinary people like us who were poor and counted for little. However, as I look back now I recognise that, although the Church as an institution was remote and irrelevant, what it represented was certainly not. What the strangeness of these buildings and people stood for was something that related to what life was about, the values that stood behind everything that was good, worthwhile and eternal.

I must have been a strange child. At one level I was the same as other working-class kids. I played football in the streets, played truant from time to time, and went scrumping (a euphemism for stealing fruit from trees, a thing I later regretted) with other teenagers to the grand houses in Upminster. I joined Barking Sea Cadets at the age of twelve and stayed four years in that wonderful organisation with weekly meetings and often sailing at weekends. Indeed, a life at sea as a radio operator was my great desire, fed by the kind of boys' stories I was reading. As far as I can remember I was popular with the other boys but my strangeness had to do with my seriousness. I was not a typical Dagenham or East End child. The war drove me to question life, its purpose, its possible meaning or futility. An element of this was in the poverty that my and many other working-class families experienced. Although our parents protected us from the harmful effects of poverty – we never went hungry – we were very aware of its shameful presence in our life and culture. There were times when Mum and Dad did miss meals in order for us to eat, and they did so gladly. But it was in other things that poverty presented itself: the clothes and shoes that were borrowed from others and the food coupons that enabled large families like ours to get a little extra. One memory stands out. The war was over and Dad wanted to get a new radio, which was our entertainment every evening. He could not afford the full cost of a new one, so it had to be obtained by hire purchase (the famous "never-never"). The agent came round to our house to speak to our parents. We children crowded around, eager to see the new wireless, as it was called then. The salesman went over the figures that Dad had given him about his wages and outgoings. Then, sighing, he closed his book and said gently to Dad: "I am sorry, Mr Carey, but you can't afford a radio yet. Perhaps in a year's time? I will keep you on the books." I still recall my emotions – of anger, of shame, of humiliation. Being resourceful, my father soon got a second-hand radio, so we continued to listen to our family programmes: *Dick Barton, Special Agent, ITMA, Much Binding in the Marsh, Round the Horne, Children's Hour*, and so on. Yet, that memory of my parents' sense of shame remains with me to this day.

My family were not political in any party sense, but we took a keen interest in what was happening nationally. Mum and Dad were working-class conservatives – a political philosophy based loosely on an unswerving love of the monarchy and the values of the Conservative Party. Dagenham in Essex was dominated by the Labour Party of which Dad had a great dislike. Sometimes I thought he was just a little bit unreasonable. I remember a moment when, about sixteen years of age, I turned on him and said: "But, Dad, what has the Conservative Party ever done for you? You have worked your fingers to the bone for your family. You have had no chance to better yourself to get a good education. You speak of the values of the Conservative Party but they have not cared for you – those rich people have done so little for you!" I believe my words may have shaken his assurance a little, but by and large, he remained firm in in his conservatism. Ironically, much later in life I found myself more at home there than elsewhere.

The income of the family left little room for luxuries like books, so the local library was a precious resource for me. As well as the great classics in the English language, I was drawn to the Philosophy and Religion section. There I discovered Bertrand Russell's great work *A History of Western Philosophy* and read it avidly and closely. This was followed by his challenging *Why I am Not a Christian*, which, interestingly, stirred my interest in issues of belief and unbelief. But I was particularly drawn to a number of Methodist writers – William Sangster and Leslie Weatherhead stand out – because of their criticism of current secular thinking and the robust way they presented a Christian faith in a way that was rich, exciting and dynamic. The war had disrupted education for many children, which left me like a starving child at a banquet of ideas. I was hooked by learning and driven to know more and more. This became a major factor in my life and all that was to follow on from my conversion to the living Christ, National Service, courtship and marriage to Eileen, ordination and all that was to come. As I have written elsewhere about these things, I will pass over these important elements in my growth to focus on the values that have shaped my ministry.

Spirituality has to be fed and nurtured. When a person starts believing, a hunger is created that has to be met by daily feeding on the Word of God and fellowship with other Christians. At the heart of my faith from the beginning has been the momentous significance and centrality of Jesus Christ. The crudely carved fish symbol found in the catacombs "ICHTHUS", the Greek letters of which stand for "Jesus Christ, Son of God, Saviour", summarised my faith – earthed in his incarnation and elevated in his resurrection and life in the Trinity. This has been the throbbing certainty of my spirituality and love of the scriptures. Indeed, there cannot be an authentic Christian faith without a strong foundation in the Bible.

I owe a great deal to the church in Dagenham where I found faith and where it was nurtured. It was also the place where Eileen and I married, and our parents are buried, and will always be a source of rich memories. The vicar, the Rev Edward Porter Conway Patterson, was an ex-missionary and had recently returned from Kenya. According to him, we were all slaves to sin and the devil stalked the land. He believed in an "inerrant" and "infallible" Bible; he hated the Roman

Catholic Church and did not have a liberal bone in his body.

But he got results. He was a fine preacher of the "fire and brimstone" variety. He inherited a good congregation from his predecessor, whom I had briefly met before his death. But "Pit-Pat", as we talked of him, drew people to the church and through his clear ministry more and more came to faith. Thursday evening was a key moment in the life of Dagenham Parish Church as we flocked to the vicarage. For thirty minutes, the vicar "opened the Word" to us and taught us the faith. It was deep stuff, thirty minutes of theology – a word never used of it, but it was there, very clearly there. And then for thirty minutes we prayed. The younger ones were expected to get on their knees, and we prayed for the nation, for the mission of the parish and for the missionary Church. There are some things that linger with you all your life and stamp it with authority; those prayer evenings still remain in my mind and heart. How I wish I could say to Pit-Pat now how much I valued that teaching and the way he made prayer so real.

However, I regret to say that there were things that I did not value, aspects that I felt were wrong and objectionable, a theology that was negative – and these sprang from Mr Patterson's deep-rooted fundamentalism. He clearly saw in the seventeen-year-old George Carey an aspiring disciple because he gave me a great deal of personal time, and lent me several books which I read avidly. But there was no room for doubt in Pit-Pat's theology. It was difficult for him to admit any deviation from a narrow conservative-evangelical viewpoint. An example was his attitude towards the Roman Catholic Church. He was especially devoted to the writings of Professor George Salmon, formerly of Trinity College, Dublin, whose massive book *The Infallibility of the Church* was very popular in nonconformist and evangelical circles.[2] My vicar gave this to me to read and I read it initially with appreciation. He often used the book in his preaching where his "knock-down" arguments were intended to show the nonsense of Roman Catholicism and all other forms of Catholicism. But the more I listened and read, the more I began to question his "certainties". My understanding was developing; I was growing in my knowledge of the Church through the ages, the faithfulness of the saints and believers of old, the courage of the monks and nuns during the so-called Dark Ages. I simply could not regard all that as superstition and mindless credulity. At the age of eighteen I was called up to do my National Service and, sadly but inevitably, my links with the vicar and church weakened. While I was abroad in Egypt and Iraq, where my call to ministry was strengthened, my contact with Mr Patterson dwindled to the occasional letter.

On my demobilisation Mr Patterson was very upset when I decided to go to the London College of Divinity (LCD) instead of an Oxbridge college. His preference was Ridley College, Cambridge, but the course at LCD and its strong links with King's, London drew me. The college offered a four-year honours degree with an emphasis upon languages. An honours student was expected to read Hebrew and Greek, which sounded a joy to me. And it was. The four years coincided with my developing romance with Eileen Hood who was embarking upon her nursing career and we married halfway through my degree course. Hensley Henson, former Bishop of Durham, once said: "Half of the clergy of the Church of England are made by their wives and the other half are undone by them." I have been totally blessed by my wife. Intelligent, humorous, tolerant, she has brought a down-to-earth godliness into our family life.

The thing about studying at any advanced level is the way it focuses your mind as well as broadens out your knowledge. It is quite wrong to believe that this means losing your cutting edge, as some Christians suggest. If the suggestion is that by studying deeply you can be in danger of becoming woolly and indistinct, then there is something very insecure about your faith. I was in no danger of that, but it did reinforce my conviction that following Jesus Christ was not a rejection of the beauty, joy and laughter of the world. Of course, Christ did challenge culture and wanted to bring it under his control, but in his earthly ministry he showed himself to be no killjoy or misery. The gospels paint a picture of a Jesus who loved life, enjoyment and the culture of his day.

I had to acknowledge to myself, even if I never told even those closest to me, that I was keenly aware that, as a largely self-taught person, there were gaps in my early education that would be difficult, if not impossible, for me to fill. Later, when visiting the top schools of the land – Eton, Winchester, St Paul's London – I realised with deep sadness that so many bright children were excluded by money from such excellence. This did not create in me anger or resentment; it instilled in me a deep longing to study, study, study and go on studying until I had mastered the subject in question. This desire for learning would later receive further satisfaction as I was able to help other "left behind" children do well at school with stronger support structures.

LCD was a great blessing to me as dedicated teachers like Hugh Jordan, Victor McCallin, Owen Brandon, Leo Stephens-Hodge and the excellent Michael Green opened my eyes to the depths of the Bible and the treasures of theology. The rhythm of worship that started at 7.15am and ended with Compline at 9.00pm and lectures throughout the day was a discipline that at times, to be frank, I complained about as too demanding. But I now feel it was an indispensable framework for life. Michael Green, a few years older than me, became a dear friend and mentor. My Greek flowered under his teaching. It was his passion for the gospel that moved this now 23-year-old and influenced me throughout my future ministry. But King's College London was also deeply satisfying. I was greatly impressed by Professor Eric Mascall, Dean of King's, whose scholarly lectures taught me so much about the history and development of theology and particularly that of Thomas Aquinas. I remember at the time thinking how ironic it was that I was being drawn into the mysterious world of "ens", "esse" and "analogia entis" – a theological landscape so anathematised by my first teacher, Mr Patterson. But "Pit-Pat" and I were not at war. He was delighted at my progress and took some delight that I was the first of seven or eight young men who went into the ordained ministry during his period of office at Dagenham Parish Church. I never left evangelicalism behind. Indeed not. I was unswervingly a gospel-centred man but I have always considered the term to indicate an embracing and inclusive concept rather than a restrictive prison. I did not feel at home in the rather narrower evangelicalism of John Stott and his near neighbour in Bishopsgate, Dick Lucas. Stott, Rector of All Souls Langham Place, was perhaps the dominant influence in the evangelical world and his clear teaching through his books and preaching was widely admired. I too admired it, but was not totally attracted to it because it seemed to allow no questions and no softening at the edges. Nevertheless, John's ministry was unquestionably significant in mainstream church life and his legacy is truly great. So it was that I sat lightly to the evangelical group, far removed from the Reformed faction, and only content with an open evangelicalism which appreciated the riches of the wider Church of England and the treasures of the Body of Christ throughout the world.

From the very beginning of my Christian life I had been nurtured by weekly gatherings with fellow believers and the daily grounding in the Bible and personal prayer. Again, I thank Pit-Pat for his influence but perhaps now, at LCD, I was beginning to consider the Bible in different ways. One cannot do serious theology without facing up to the questions that emerge from the sacred texts themselves and which generations of scholars have considered in detail. After all, there are four gospels, not one, and there are significant differences between the gospels. The fourth gospel – the spiritual gospel – is so unlike the synoptic gospels (Mark, Matthew and Luke) that fundamental questions confront the honest scholar.

The same goes for the first part of the Bible which we call the Old Testament but is more accurately described as the Hebrew scriptures, because they are first and foremost the holy books of the Jews. The questions are formidable: creation in seven days – is that believable? Indeed not, in the light of scientific progress since the days of Charles Darwin. Wide discrepancies exist in the books that focus on the history of Israel, the Chronicles and the books called Kings. I quickly realised that one could not skip over these differences as though they did not exist. Serious scholarship going back years had studied the different types of literature in the Old

17

Testament. That scholarship could not be rejected; it had to be critically studied and mastered. There was no obvious unity to the Hebrew scriptures – and, as well as the historical books of the Old Testament, there are poetry, prophecy and at least three types of law. If one then applies terms like "infallibility" and "inerrancy" to the text of the Bible major intellectual issues arise.

I could not in all honesty dismiss such questions as irrelevant. Instead, I concluded that the only Word of God is the one proclaimed in John 1: "In the beginning was the Word, and the Word was with God and the Word was God." Jesus is the revealed Word of God. The scriptures point to him. How then did I interpret the scriptures? Not as infallible writings but faithful writings that the church had inherited and which spoke of His faithfulness to the Hebrew people and then to us, the followers of Jesus called the Christ. Not that this solved all the problems, but it did at least allow honest disciples to explore those differences in the text. To those who think that this minimises the value of the Bible and reduces its significance I can only respond with incredulity. Far from it, I am often amazed by the way the Bible questions me and my sin and fallen-ness. As for all the questions about the infallibility or inerrancy of scripture, I was wholly content with the conclusion expressed by Article VI of the Book of Common Prayer that "the Holy Scriptures contains all things necessary to salvation". The point of the Bible is that it feeds us. In the lapidary words of Gregory the Great: "Scripture is like a river, broad and deep, shallow enough here for the lamb to go wading, but deep enough there for the elephant to swim."[3]

An example of my differences from some in the evangelical world was when John Stott, much later, accepted my invitation to spend a weekend at St Nicholas's Durham. He was a delightful guest. I remember our children being fascinated by his focus on a daily HHH. What is a HHH, they asked? John gave the reply that every day one should have a rest after lunch: "It is my 'horizontal half hour," he responded and explained that it was part of his daily discipline. Later, when we were together in my study, John said that he valued my book *I Believe in Man* but he regretted deeply that I had expressed my belief in evolution which, he said, was unbiblical and a theory only.[4] We had a deep discussion in which I expressed my view that there could be very little doubt that Darwin's theory was substantially correct. I explained that Genesis 1-3 was parabolic in nature and surely, it was not written to describe how the world was created? Our conversation did not result in agreement, but did end very cordially. Nonetheless, John Stott was a huge success that weekend at St Nic's and the largely student congregation hung upon his every word. I saw John several times when I was Archbishop and then, finally, at the College of St Barnabas, Lingfield, where his final years were spent. We had a delightful time together in which I was able to thank him for his outstanding ministry.

Returning to my development as a scholar, Eric Mascall later went on to examine me for my Master's in Theology, which I did at King's. I think he was delighted that this young evangelical was keen to receive his guidance. I had found in his writings a depth and spirituality that deepened my understanding of God. The Catholic writers of the past inspired Eric's theology and worship. I remember my final meeting with him shortly before Christmas 1963 when I sat my viva for the M.Th. Another examiner was with him. The questioning was thorough and tough but the mood of the examination seemed to suggest that they were reasonably content with my thesis. I was aching to know if I had passed, but I could not ask that directly. Professor Mascall must have read my mind. He walked me to the door and holding my hand for a very long time and looking directly at me said, "You will have a very happy Christmas." I stammered a heartfelt "thank you" and went home to tell a joyful Eileen.

It was in my final year at College that Eileen and I faced a huge blow – we lost our first child. We had been delighted when we learned she was pregnant in the second year of our marriage. Eileen was at that point staff nurse in the radiotherapy unit at Mount Vernon hospital. She had a healthy pregnancy and worked for most of the time in a post that gave her huge personal satisfaction. However, we became rather worried that at full term she was still awaiting the birth. Sixteen further days passed and the hospital called her in. After examination we were told there was no heartbeat and our baby was dead. There followed a long, induced labour after which my brave and beautiful wife of just twenty-two gave birth to a dead little boy. Until then we had hardly heard of the term "stillbirth" and the hospital certainly had no formal procedures for parents in our situation. The staff nurse, a warm-hearted Irish woman, tried to offer words of comfort that our little boy was in limbo and safe in the arms of God. This theology made little sense to me, I thought at the time. I held this beautiful little boy in my arms, but his mother was accorded no such joy. No chaplain was summoned to pray with us. Our son was taken from us and laid to rest in Hillingdon cemetery. We were given a number. We named him Stephen and ever since April 2nd has been a date scarred in our memory to be remembered annually. We returned home deeply, deeply traumatised by being so abandoned by the hospital. Once more Michael and Rosemary Green were helpful in their care and support. This event brought home to us both that Christians have no special "get out of jail free" card when it comes to life's struggles.

The next step for us was parish ministry which I loved. Our time at St Mary's Islington, London, under the leadership of Peter Johnston and Phyllis, his wife, provided us both with an excellent grounding for all that was to follow. Peter had only taken over leadership of St Mary's two years earlier from Maurice Wood. Peter had been a late ordinand, having had a career in the Royal Navy. I think Peter compared himself unfavourably with his predecessor because of his lack of a degree. How sad it is that lack of academic success, largely because of circumstances, leads some to believe they are inferior. There was nothing inferior about Peter. He was a shrewd, competent pastor, a good preacher and he built up the congregation at St Mary's in Upper Street. From Peter I learned the importance of spending time with people – that pastoral ministry is not secondary to preaching but that both belong together.

It was a large clergy team with four curates. Each of us was expected to make twenty visits to homes each week, which may sound easy but is, in fact, very hard to fit in. Add to this all the cups of tea you were expected to drink. This caused me to give up sugar in my tea and I never resumed it. From Peter I learned to love people, to listen to them, visit them regularly, keep your promises to them and never fail them. Visiting people in Islington in the 1960s was a real eye-opener because of the degree of poverty. St Mary's attracted the professional classes but found it a struggle to get people from the flats and tiny, cramped and cluttered houses to come to church. This has always been a problem for the English Church, and I have always been sceptical of the saying that "a house-visiting pastor makes a church-going people". That was certainly not true in my experience, but what visiting did do was to bring the church into the home. I found it a great pleasure to visit the flats and to be known by the families and children. I started a boys' football team and this drew in some of the dads to help with training on a Saturday morning. We even played games on the famous Hackney Marshes with other youth teams. One of the results was that the Sunday School was swelled by youngsters from the flats who had, initially, more interest in games than Bible stories.

Looking back I have no doubt that the time spent visiting and becoming known in the parish was time well spent. But times change and, even though I carried on that practice when vicar of St Nic's Durham, I wonder whether such discipline would work now in the 2020s. Perhaps not with so many households empty during the day. The sadness is that clergy have become invisible and remote from the lives of parishioners. Finding ways of bridging that gap must be one of the most important challenges facing the church today.

The four years at St Mary's Church learning from Peter were a real blessing for Eileen and myself. Three of our children were born there and Eileen as an energetic young woman flowered under the tutelage of Phyllis Johnston. I shudder even now when I think with shame of the way the Church then treated women. No woman was expected to enter the sanctuary and it was accepted that women could not be ordained. There was one woman on the staff team,

Doreen Bergernie, who was then in her early thirties. She was called "the lady worker". A single woman, Doreen was a RADA-trained actress – clever, sophisticated and very articulate – but was considered inferior to men in her ministry. Perhaps it was then that my desire to see women ordained was born, because I could see no clear reason why theologically and scripturally women could not be ordained. If the Spirit falls on all people, women as well as men (Joel 2:29), then gender cannot be a problem. But Doreen herself accepted the restrictions and never complained. She was a marvellous member of our team and I learned so many things from her.

As for Eileen, aged twenty-three when I was ordained deacon, she brought up our three older children in a tiny damp cottage, with no washing machine, tumble dryer or other mod cons. We were very poor and had no car, although Sheila Moore, a parishioner, gave us the use of her car for our days off. But we were content and true to each other. That another woman could take her place was out of the question, not only because of my deep love for her but also because of my ordination vows. "Be holy, for I am holy" is the pulsating command of the Almighty and central to the ordained ministry (Leviticus 11:44-45; 1 Peter 1:15-16). Of course, as with everyone else in a loving relationship with another, there have been ups and downs in that marital relationship. We have had arguments, most of them trivial and, on a few occasions, serious rifts that may have lasted a few days. But there has been no momentous blow-up that has seriously questioned our love for each other. And when tensions have occurred, I am sure it has largely been my fault through neglect and indifference. And perhaps it is not only our common faith and love that have kept us together, but also our children and our responsibilities towards them.

After four happy years at St Mary's we moved to Oakhill Theological College. This was a rather serendipitous moment because I had no intention of going into theological education. I had assumed that I would do another curacy after Islington but this was not to be. A year earlier Maurice Wood, the Principal, had phoned Peter Johnston to ask if he would release George Carey to help with teaching part of the degree course, as a lecturer was very ill and there was a need for assistance. Thus, in my third year at St Mary's I did a few hours teaching at Oakhill and enjoyed it greatly. I must have impressed Maurice sufficiently to be invited for a full-time post. But moving from the parish was a huge wrench. I loved the activity and life of the parish: the wonderful London parishioners, the different ethnic groups and the deep fellowship of the clergy team. I was slightly fearful of working intensively with an academic team under the leadership of the very popular and charismatic Maurice Wood.

It turned out there was nothing to fear. Maurice could not have been more charming and supportive of this now 29-year-old. I was actually younger than many of the student body who had received the call of ordination later in life. And now began one of the happiest learning periods of my life. The staff team was strong academically and motivated. John Taylor, a Hebrew scholar, taught Old Testament. John would later become a greatly loved Bishop of St Albans. John Simpson taught liturgy and worship and would become Dean of Canterbury where we would meet and work together later. David Field taught ethics and became a good friend. Alan Holloway taught history and worked night and day, so much so that his constant refrain was "I'm so tired!" My closest colleague, who became a lifelong friend, was Philip Crowe. Philip, who was the same age as me, and his wife Freda lived next door and our young families grew up together. It was at Oakhill that I completed my Ph.D. As I look back now I am still amazed how I found the time to teach New Testament and theology at an advanced level, be a dad, be a husband and complete a doctorate. The explanation was partly in Eileen's support and encouragement but also that, at that age, one's capacity to work, and to do so on just a few hours' sleep, is boundless.

However, there was a mystery to solve. In my last year at St Mary's someone had stuffed an envelope through our letter box. Within it was £100 with a note: "To register for the Ph.D." Back then that was a huge sum of money. Thus encouraged I registered and pressed on. But who was the mysterious donor and encourager? We had no idea at the time. I found out much later that it was Phyllis Johnston who did not wish to be thanked – however, we were able to do so before her death.

Oakhill was formative in all kinds of ways. We enjoyed the social life and the intense working relationships with staff and students. The teaching was exciting and not as narrow as reputed. However, it did make me aware that in a number of ways my thinking was less conservative than my colleagues at Oakhill. I found myself uncomfortable with interpreting the Christian faith through the prism of a rather narrow evangelicalism. The breadth and richness of a faith fed from Catholic, Orthodox, charismatic as well as the evangelical tradition excited me.

I was in the Oakhill football team and enjoyed the physical activity of playing together against other teams in our league. London Bible College was by far the best footballing side, followed by Spurgeons, the Baptist college. Later in life I reflected on the fact that my ecumenical experience began on the football field and in the tea afterwards. Friendly theological exchanges usually followed with heated discussion around points of contention. Friendship is, of course, the precondition of true dialogue and meeting of hearts.

Theological colleges are never remote from the world or the Church. They are integrated in the life of the national church and staff are expected to contribute through their writings and scholarship. In my second year at Oakhill the National Evangelical Anglican Congress met at Keele University. John Stott was the convenor and chairman and there was much excitement and expectation as the conference drew near. I was not directly involved and, indeed, was reluctant to get drawn in. I was completing my Ph.D. and had a very heavy teaching load. Philip Crowe, however, was very closely involved in the planning and, especially during the conference, in the writing up of the reports and conclusions. Although John Stott was the *éminence grise* of NEAC and led it with clarity and Pope-like authority, it was largely a young men's conference with people like Colin Buchanan, Gavin Reid, Philip Crowe and others in their thirties taking the initiative and blazing a trail. Indeed, NEAC could even be described as a "coming of age" for the conservative evangelical tradition. John Stott made the same point when he declared that "nothing comparable has been attempted within living memory, if ever before". Without exaggeration it was a turning point in the history of Anglican evangelicalism. I managed to get away from my normal responsibilities to attend for just one day and the excitement and euphoria were captivating. It was, of course, echoing the ferment going on in society generally with the revolution in music through the Beatles and Rolling Stones, plus the disturbing student rebellion in Paris and elsewhere. In Rome the on-going Second Vatican Council was beginning to change the face, if not the nature, of Roman Catholicism, and impact other Christian bodies. One observer, indeed, likened NEAC to the Second Vatican Council, breathing a spirit of *aggiornamento* through the Church of England. However, unlike Vatican II, NEAC was not doing a "root and branch" examination of the faith of the Church but, rather, it represented a real engagement with the rest of the Church of England in a spirit of cooperation and service. In an article for the *Church Times* John Stott admitted that he hoped that "the Congress will gain us greater respect in the Church as a whole". It certainly did that and the fact that the Archbishop of Canterbury, Michael Ramsey, opened the Congress with a powerful and friendly speech affirming the central truths of evangelicalism, represented a real meeting of hearts. However, looking back I find myself asking: what did Keele actually achieve? In fact, there was nothing earth-shaking in the 10,000-word Declaration that emerged from Keele. There was no attempt to change doctrine but there was a strong affirmation of the identity of evangelicals in terms of evangelical truths: the supremacy of scripture, the majesty of Jesus Christ, the Lordship of the Holy Spirit, the necessity of conversion, the priority of evangelism and the importance of the Church. However, NEAC was a major step forward in the life of the Church of England as the majority of evangelical clergy and laity committed themselves, with renewed confidence and with determination, to be a positive force in the Church.

In 1969 Michael Green, Principal of London College of Divinity, asked me to join his staff as the college moved from Northwood to a site close to Nottingham University. It was a very tempting proposition not simply because of my friendship with Michael but also because of what it represented in terms of experimenting with theological education. I knew that Michael was keen to blend academic excellence with a down-to-earth approach to evangelism. I was flattered by the invitation but also slightly guilty about leaving Oakhill for another college in the same tradition. I need not have worried; Maurice was understanding and charming. I had had slight differences with him and his approach to theology, but he had been a warm and approachable boss. Also leaving Oakhill and going with me to St John's Nottingham, as it was going to be called, was John Goldingay, who taught Old Testament alongside John Taylor. John Goldingay was some seven years my junior and an impressive scholar. Mischievously, at our farewell I was able to incorporate a verse from Genesis (22:5) in my speech where Abraham says to the servants, "Stay here with the ass while I and the lad go yonder!" Maurice roared with laughter because there was no malice behind my misuse of the text. Years later, on my becoming Archbishop, Maurice was generous enough to present me with a pair of buckled shoes, which he knew I would have to buy for special royal occasions. I was able to thank him for his tolerance of my younger and more impulsive self. It was a royal gift indeed.

2

Learning to Lead

Never doubt that a small group of thoughtful, concerned citizens can change the world. Indeed it is the only thing that ever has.

Margaret Mead

From 1970 to 1975 Eileen and I had a quite different experience at St John's College, Nottingham. It was an exciting five years of sharing with a different staff and a young body of students. We loved Oakhill but it was far more formal and sedate than St John's. Formerly my old college, London College of Divinity, now relocated to Nottingham, St John's was still a building site when we moved in. Our children had to climb over piles of rock and stumble up unmade roads to get to school. At first staff and students had to improvise in classrooms when the lights did not function or the heating system was cut off for periods.

But what an exciting time it was. Michael Green assembled around himself a staff he trusted, who shared his vision to develop a college that was contemporary, relevant and focused on the modern world. Colin Buchanan, Julian Charley, Anne Long, Charles Napier, Noel Pollard, John Goldingay, Franklyn Dulley, Gordon Jones and

Stephen Travis were also part of this team and we forged a close and affirming teaching team that was exciting to belong to. Colin Buchanan would later become a dear friend. It was a very talented staff; we argued a lot and laughed a great deal. But it was a huge privilege to be part of Michael's team. Both Eileen and I were delighted to be bringing up our three children – Rachel, Mark and Andrew – in such a friendly and secure college campus. We welcomed into the world our fourth child, Lizzie, in 1971 while we were at St John's.

The unspoken philosophy of the college lay in its commitment to an open evangelicalism – open to the needs of the world and particularly to the Holy Spirit. Besides Michael, two other members of the staff were acquiring a national reputation for their advanced thinking. Colin Buchanan was at the cutting edge of liturgical studies and was a very popular speaker. Julian Charley, Vice Principal, was forging a positive image for the evangelical tradition by his commitment to ecumenism and he was later appointed a member of the Anglican-Roman Catholic International Commission (ARCIC). Others of us were also reaching out beyond the narrow confines of the college to the wider Church. As a former Catholic theologian, Charles Napier, a dearly beloved member of the team, brought a contemplative dimension that added to the rich mix of the staff.

The period coincided with the advent of the Charismatic Movement that was shaking and "disturbing" all mainstream churches. St John's welcomed this new movement of the Spirit openly. However, some of us were sceptical about the idea of a second baptism in the Holy Spirit because of the divisive implications of having a superior class of people who spoke in tongues. Charles Napier, who also taught theology, and I were vocally opposed and there were several open debates where our arguments were expressed in friendly yet strong discussions. As time went on we all learned that the real significance of the Charismatic Movement lay in less controversial things: that all Christians have gifts to use for God, that music does not have to be staid or boring, that all should be open to the Spirit of God. John V. Taylor, Bishop of Winchester, was one of the first theologians to observe what was going on in his seminal book, *The*

Go-Between God.[5] "We are all meant to possess our possessions," he wrote, "but many never do." That is to say, that God the Spirit longs for us all to deepen our experience of the faith and to know his power and freedom.

The Charismatic Movement was indeed a very powerful influence in all churches, including the Roman Catholic Church. No doubt, here and there, it was divisive but in the life of St John's Theological College it was positive and healing. Whilst most of us on the faculty were initially disposed to frown upon it and dismiss it, we had to acknowledge the benefits of its influence. Indeed, it had a profound impact on me because, for some seven or eight years cut off from the real life of parish ministry, college life was like being in the back room of an army support organisation, providing weapons for others but not experiencing the front-line life of a soldier. I cannot deny the real blessing this brought to me personally as I opened myself to the power of the Holy Spirit. The Bible took on a new relevance and depth of meaning. I began to see new ways through the Charismatic Movement to empower the Church and renew Christian mission. It was this that convinced me that, after five years at St John's, it was time to go back into a parish.

St Nicholas' Durham was to be that parish, where we served for seven happy but extremely hard years, from 1975 to 1982. I have written about this experience in *The Church in the Market Place*.[6] A traditional evangelical church, St Nic's had a mainly student ministry served by our namesakes, George and Eileen Marchant, who had been at the helm of the church for twenty years. They were lovely, caring and devoted people and George's long ministry at St Nic's had been noted for its teaching ministry.

I was thirty-nine years of age and in too much of a hurry. I could see what I wanted to do, but my initial mistake was to try to do things too quickly. As I look back, I see that the initial changes I made were not that earth-shattering. I brought in more Communion services, new hymns, a music group because there was no choir – but I failed to prepare the ground well or explain my intentions. I lost over twenty people because of my enthusiasm and eagerness to get things done. Although, later, after the changes to the building, some of them returned, I regretted the lack of care for a few elderly people who loved their church and felt as though they were forced to leave. I have often asked myself, would they have ever accepted what I wanted to do even with the full backing of the Church Council? I suspect not, but to this day I rue the fact that I did not spend more time with this group of people. This was a lesson I learned and took on into other spheres of work; it boiled down to the importance of listening to others and attempting to bring the most reluctant opponents of new things into the centre of discussions.

The church premises were in an awful state. It was, I was told by the archdeacon, the last church in the diocese still to have a coal burner and the fumes darkened the church and had us all coughing on a Sunday. Every Saturday evening I had to borrow six oil-fed heaters to supplement the ailing coal boiler, which hardly made a difference at all during the long Durham winters. Something had to be done – and we launched an appeal to raise £2,000 for a new heating system for the church. On hearing this the Church Treasurer resigned, saying that "it couldn't be done!" How often I have heard that over the years. Church members, however, were surprised at how quickly the money was raised.

While that was going on I was very exercised about what I wanted St Nic's to be. I had a sketch of something in my head and on the Church Council we had several discussions about the ministry of the church on this distinctive site, at the entrance to the cathedral and colleges. Indeed, I took the question of the relevance of the church into the world around. I spoke to several business and professional people who worked in the market square. A meeting with the Town Clerk was memorable. The town hall was adjacent to the church and the Town Clerk's office overlooked the porch of St Nicholas'. He offered me a coffee and listened to my questions about the ministry of the church. He then took me to the window where we could see people in the square below. There was no one near the porch. "I don't know what you could or should do," he said, "but if you don't do something soon, that building will be closed in twenty years' time, or end up as a shop." Considering that a church had stood on that site for over one thousand years, his comment was a shocking and grim thing to hear. I was determined that we would not succumb that easily.

The Town Clerk was not the only "outsider" I asked for thoughts on what the church could become. The market square is full of shops and businesses in competition, seeking to sell and be successful. I knew that some of the business leaders would have reflections on that strange, old building in the corner. And that was the case. I found a great deal of interest, and people were not indifferent to the Christian faith. A number of them expressed their desire that St Nic's might become a bustling place at the heart of the square. Indeed, we began to explore this in terms of mission. Among the many students who came every Sunday were Alison and Mark, both talented actors. I asked them to help me in portraying Bible stories and ordinary events to illustrate my addresses. This led to me offering them a contract for two years in which they became staff members and exercised a powerful ministry. Alison eventually married Frank White and later went on to be ordained and eventually Bishop of Hull.

It was a layman, Dr Gerald Blake, a lecturer in geography at the university, who was to advance our thinking. He asked to meet me over coffee and he sketched out an idea of a building which never closed its doors – a church with a shop, offering food for the homeless, with moveable furniture to be entirely accessible to groups who wished to use our facilities, attractive, bright and modern. Instantly I knew that Gerald was on to something and, together, we shared the idea with a small group from the Church Council. The concept developed and with the help of a gifted architect from York, Ronald Sims, the vision took shape and eventually was launched as our major building project. But no leader, and certainly no clergyman, can achieve much without the effective contribution of others and I was most fortunate to have a lay team of exceptional ability: Peter Green, John Ledger, Peter West, Richard Briggs, David Day and many others. At different times I had the support of two able curates, Pete Broadbent and Frank White, who later went on to become bishops.

I have described the challenges in my book *The Church in the Market Place*. It was a time of great stress for me as vicar. It brought home in a stark way the, at times, unbearable weight of being a leader. Although I was supported well by a strong lay team, a leader is ultimately alone. But a Christian leader has one enormous advantage over others and that is the strength of faith and the way that one's spirituality underpins the role of a leader. Without in any way distancing myself from the evangelical tradition I was gaining much from other traditions, Anglo-Catholic, Methodist and Roman Catholic. Faith builds up. I was invited to Ushaw Roman Catholic College and was delighted to meet Fr John Redford who had been a student at the London College of Theology when I was there. He was one year my senior, so we had not been in the same group but the whole student body had been profoundly shocked when we heard that in his diaconate he had become a Roman Catholic. Back then it was anathema to many of our contemporaries. Now a theologian and teacher, John and I were able to greet each other as good friends and our friendship was renewed. We met and shared often after that. I recalled Pit-Pat's antagonism towards Catholics and was thankful that even as a young Christian I had not gone down that road.

In November 1976 I received a call from Christopher Hill, one of the Archbishop of Canterbury's officers (later to become Bishop of Guildford), asking if I would like to represent the Church of England as part of an Anglican team in Rome on a three-week visit to the Anglican Centre. I was stunned as well as excited. As I looked out from my study across a cold and wet Durham nothing seemed more appealing than spending three weeks in Rome the next spring. Following the impact of Vatican II and the visit of Archbishop Michael Ramsey to Rome as guest of Pope Paul VI, the desire of both churches was to seek full and visible unity, which we knew was the longing of our Lord. That visit was to have a profound impact on my life.

February 1977 was a wild month in Durham but it was almost spring-like when a party of some thirty young men, led by Bishop John Moorman, settled in Rome as guests of the Anglican Centre.

We were welcomed by the director, Fr Harry Smythe, and asked to introduce ourselves. We represented most of the provinces of the Anglican Communion. There then began an intensive programme of theological study, interspersed by lectures of the highest quality. The primary aim was to get younger Anglican clergy engaged with Roman Catholic theology and thinking. I was deeply impressed by the quality of the other Anglicans, particularly Bishop Misaeri Kauma, Assistant Bishop of Namirembe, in Uganda. Misaeri and I became instant friends and shared deeply together especially when we heard the news, whilst we were there, that his Archbishop, Janani Luwum, had been murdered by Idi Amin. Among the lecturers were Terry Waite, then working for a Roman Catholic missionary agency, Father Bernard Häring, a moral theologian of international reputation, and Professor Gerry O'Collins, Professor of Systematic and Fundamental Theology at the Pontifical Gregorian University. I was particularly drawn towards Gerry, an open and friendly Australian, and our friendship continues to this day. Gerry's powerful book, *Fundamental Theology*,[7] showed me how much overlap there is between Roman Catholic theology and Anglicanism. Gerry became a personal friend not only because of the nature of his teaching but also because of his attractive personal faith. He was a happy Christian, always laughing, smiling and showing the attractive character of a life that brought together a living faith and commitment to the world around. Our group enjoyed a personal audience with Pope Paul VI who chatted to each one of us personally and answered questions later. One fact which interested me greatly was to note the deep divisions in the Roman Catholic Church. Father Häring represented a more liberal strand in the Catholic Church, as indeed did Professor Karl Jung who later became a close friend. In Rome I came across as many different types of Catholics as there are types of Anglicans. I took some comfort from that, because differences should not spell division.

Three weeks is but a short time but it represented a spiritual revolution in my life and heart. I returned home deeply affirmed in my ecumenical convictions, strongly convinced that, though

Anglicans were estranged from Rome, Catholics and Anglicans along with other mainstream Christian denominations were bound together by a common faith. I vowed to carry on thinking deeply about the things I had gained during those precious three weeks. Indeed, two years later I returned to Rome on my own for three weeks to carry on studying – this time a study focused on the Blessed Virgin Mary. This was another rich time of renewal, reflection and study.

Returning to St Nic's after that heady experience meant plunging headlong into the renewal of church life and into the building programme. It was an amazing adventure as well as a deeply humbling one as God answered prayer and as lives were changed. I was able to see that a very important element of growth lay in the unity and cohesion of the congregation. Such cohesion is related to the sense of purpose, which in the case of St Nic's was initially seen in the building project but would later grow into a definite mission to reach out and assist others. In this women and men pulled together. Eileen was deeply involved in the Wives Fellowship and the catering team.

But it was far from easy. It was exhausting and very worrying as we were trying to raise hundreds of thousands of pounds at a time when inflation was 18 per cent. However, we achieved it and the church was opened by the Bishop of Durham, John Habgood, in November 1981. We chose a novel way of dedicating the church: the bishop processed to different parts of the building and we all crowded around the bishop as he led us in prayer. John said later that this was the first time he had blessed and dedicated the toilets of a church. What a time of rejoicing the completion of the improvements represented. I had no doubt that the whole team had saved the ministry of St Nic's for future generations to enjoy and share with others. It also brought home to me the nature of faith, which is only known and experienced as we embark upon it.

The phone rang. It was a Monday morning in December 1981, and the caller was someone from Trinity College, Bristol. I was asked if I would allow my name to go forward for consideration as the next Principal of Trinity. I replied that, attractive as the offer was, I was not in any position to consider it as my job was certainly not over at St Nic's. The caller pleaded with me to reconsider and I firmly said "no". But the calls persisted with the Chairman of the Council phoning who asked if I would be prepared to visit Trinity to see the college. This seemed quite madness from one point of view. The job was not over at St Nic's because, although the building work was complete, we needed to pay off the remainder of costs and put the vision into practice. I had no intention of handing over this magnificent project to another. Nevertheless Eileen and I considered the request from Trinity carefully, as I had promised. Eileen was adamantly opposed to any move, as much for the sake of our own sanity as well as the welfare of our children. As we have always done, we shared this problem with the senior church leaders and the view was that I should, at least, go to see the college.

I went quite cheerfully because I was convinced that there was really no call in the invitation. How wrong I was. I found myself sitting with the entire College Council going through what seemed like an interview situation. It was clear that the college was in a challenging position. Although it was called "Trinity" to emphasise the unity of three disparate colleges – Tyndale, Clifton and St Michael's, the women's college – the unity was wafer thin and deep divisions were present in the council. But that was not all. The college body comprised only about fifty students. To break even financially, the college needed to have well over seventy students. The college, in short, was broke. But I could not deny the attractiveness of the challenge. The only way was up in this dire situation. I was rocked to find out during the day that the council had indeed set this up as an interview because I met an archdeacon at lunchtime who had also been called to meet the council. At the end of the day I was offered the position as Principal of Trinity College as from the autumn of 1982.

I returned home rather disturbed. There was no doubt that Trinity was in a parlous situation, run down to a serious degree. But I felt a sense of call towards this fresh challenge and to my surprise

Eileen felt it also. The Church Council was consulted, both of us having agreed that, if the Council as a body felt otherwise, I would reject the offer from Trinity. However, they were all supportive and felt that I was ready for another monumental challenge.

A monumental challenge it certainly was. The staff team of Trinity was a talented and united body – Dr Peter Williams, Gerry Angel, Joy Tetley, John Wesson and others – learned and very able people, but there was no disguising deep problems that would soon end the college if not dealt with. Under my predecessors an emphasis had been given to receiving students from overseas, many of them admirers of Jim Packer, whose theology, rooted in the Puritan tradition, was very popular in evangelical circles. However, ringing in my ears were words offered to me by the Bishop of Durham, John Habgood, "We want you to bring Trinity back into the Church of England." And that was my intention. I was certainly not opposed to the evangelicalism of Jim Packer, a theologian I admired greatly, but I regarded it as a strand untypical of mainstream Anglicanism.

The first problem was the unity of Trinity. The trustees of Clifton Theological College, which was the principal building of the three properties, were in no hurry to hand over the deeds of the building, so, essentially, Trinity did not own the main building. I found the lay trustees suspicious of the new Principal and unwilling to cooperate. It was clear that I had to build up trust and befriend them, which would take time. It did. Indeed, some fifteen months passed before the trustees felt sufficiently happy with me and the way the college was going to relinquish control of the Clifton site.

In the meantime, the task consisted in building up the student body, recruiting and encouraging belief in Trinity and its values. I found the task bore an uncanny likeness to what the St John's team had been doing under Michael Green, some twelve years earlier. But the quality of the incoming students delighted me and the staff team. Many of them were in their late twenties with young families, and Eileen formed a wives' group for mutual encouragement and support. Women students of ability started arriving, largely encouraged by Archbishop Robert Runcie's initiative to allow women to be deacons. However, here I encountered a difficulty that I was not prepared for. Sunday evenings were reserved for students to get experience in preaching in selected parishes in the area. I was shocked when a very able young woman in her late twenties was refused permission to preach in a local church. The tutor responsible for the group of students came to me with the problem and I phoned the church warden in charge, as that church was in an interregnum. The man refused to budge: "We do not welcome women deacons or priests here," he argued. There was little I could do and I had to pass on the news to the upset student. But sometimes events take an unexpected turn that could almost be called "divine intervention". The replacement preacher, a young man, became sick on the day before the sermon. We had no choice but to ask for the same young woman to stand in on the Sunday evening. The following day I received a subdued phone call from the church warden. "She was superb and we were all bowled over by her presence and preaching. From now on we will have no objection to women preachers." While that was excellent news in that case, as the movement for women's ordination grew in intensity, the same prejudice was encountered again and again. I knew, as someone totally committed to the ordination of women, that the battle had to be mounted on two fronts – theological and experience. Later I would be overcome by joy as, on my watch as Archbishop, women would be allowed ordination to the priesthood.

The five years we spent at Trinity were amongst the happiest of my ministry. The number of students continued to rise until Trinity became the largest college in the Church of England. We even started a new building project for the growing numbers of students. The teaching I did was not onerous because my role was in leading and building up the college, but it was truly a time of learning and sharing. Leadership is rarely about dominating; it is essentially about keeping one's eye on the goal and encouraging others to share in the vision. I have often called leadership "the art of making things possible". It does not matter who gets the credit – so often the obstacle that gets in the way of growth – but that we achieve together what we most desire.

The final Saturday of June 1987 was a very hot day which coincided with a celebration of Trinity's work and a farewell to final year students. A marquee had been erected on the front lawn and the service was led by the Chair of the council, the Rev Roy Henderson, the greatly respected vicar of St Mary's Stoke Bishop. As he spoke I was immediately conscious that the fulsome words he was saying about the college's success included me. I became embarrassed because he was speaking as though I were leaving. I glanced across at Eileen who raised her eyebrows in astonishment also. There was no time to inquire about this at the time because priority had to be given to the leavers and their families. It was a truly happy occasion.

The following Monday explained it all as a letter from No. 10 Downing Street offered me the bishopric of Bath and Wells on the retirement of John Bickersteth. Now I understand, I said to myself. Jill Dann, a member of the College Council and also a member of the Crown Appointments Committee, had obviously given the signal to Roy Henderson. I was shocked. Sincerely I did not long for preferment in the Church of England. I was expecting the next post after being Principal of Trinity would be back in parish ministry. I have never been an ambitious person and it was with much regret that Eileen and I within a few months had to move from Bristol to the lovely city of Wells, the smallest city in England. And from parish priest and principal to Bishop of Bath and Wells – rather a step for a child from the East End of London and Dagenham, Essex.

But one member of our family was distinctly displeased: our sixteen-year-old daughter Elizabeth. She loved Bristol and had a wide coterie of friends. "Wells is full of old people!" was her verdict before even visiting the place. But it did not take her long to realise what a hasty judgment that was. It was there that she found her vocation to be a nurse and would spend many years in the area, serving others.

Settling into the Bishop's Palace was a rather surreal experience. Since Bishop "Jock" Henderson's times in the 1960s the bishop had lived in the servants' quarters rather than the main house. That had been a good decision which allowed tourists to visit the moated palace and enjoy the beauty of the place. It was a perfect place for the work of a modern bishop with entertaining as a major component of what he had to do.

The staff team I inherited was quite superb, with Nigel McCulloch, Bishop of Taunton, and three outstanding archdeacons plus the Dean of the Cathedral, Patrick Mitchell. They were truly supportive and wonderful colleagues. But I was itching to get into the parishes to support and encourage the clergy and it was important to get to know them first. With the help of Mary Masters, my energetic and talented secretary, we set about visiting all clergy in their homes. Eileen was delighted to be part of this and for the first six months we visited clergy families every weekday, five or six families a week. It was exhausting work but delightful, rewarding – and humbling: humbling because for a significant number of the clergy the rewards for sacrificial work were sometimes indifference, ingratitude and sheer slog. Some of the villages had few inhabitants and a number of the churches were unheated and consequently ill-suited for modern times when people expected comfort and mod cons. But the opportunities for growth were there for outgoing and ambitious clergy and I was excited when I saw a number of initiatives that looked well for the future.

My very first confirmation on Sunday, February 21st 1988 will long stand out in my memory for its comedy, as well as for its reassurance. St Andrew's Church, High Ham, is a beautiful pre-Reformation church and I made sure I got there in good time to run over the programme with the vicar and meet those being confirmed – a group of twelve of mixed ages. I was using a crozier specially made for me by a friend, carved from local Somerset wood. It was in two parts for the ease of packing and travelling around the diocese. What I did not know was that, as I walked up the aisle, the bottom part had dropped off. As I approached the altar after the actual confirmation I became conscious that the choir were beside themselves with laughter, and titters of merriment were coming from the congregation. I looked back and could see that the Rev

Peter Coney, acting as my chaplain, was holding the bottom part of the crozier and I, ridiculously, was holding the top part! My embarrassment turned to laughter as I saw the funny side of it. It was a wonderful moment as the dignity, pomp and ceremony were taken up into the celebration of the ordinary.

But that first confirmation service was also very reassuring. To be honest, I had not been looking forward to wearing cope and mitre and processing around looking like something from *Alice in Wonderland*. Although it seemed to go well, in spite of, or because of, the crozier, I was eager to know if I had done it properly. In the vestry, alone with Peter Coney, as we divested, I asked, "Well, Peter, that was my first confirmation. How did it go?"

Peter must have realised that, as a new bishop, I needed reassurance. He put his hand on my arm and said: "Bishop George. When you were appointed we wanted you, not a particular sort of bishop. Be yourself!" Peter, who became a dear and trusted friend, said something that evening which has stayed with me forever.

However, I was not content with the tradition of instituting clergy and confirmations that every bishop was expected to do. Although I was delighted to carry on such activities wholeheartedly, I was dissatisfied. They were too traditional and did not match up to what I expected a missionary bishop to be and do. The growing secularisation of society, it seemed to me, demanded a fresh approach in which the bishop was required to lead the "mission of the people of God". We had to leave our comfortable episcopal studies and "get out there". I, therefore, created an outreach team of musicians, dramatists and lay leaders to go with me into deaneries and parishes for five days at a time. I had no idea if anyone would be interested in the idea, so I was overwhelmed by the enthusiasm that greeted these "missions". The first parish and group of churches to show interest was that of St John the Baptist, Wellington in the south of the diocese. The vicar, Terry Stokes, was a tall, sophisticated Anglo-Catholic who had no problem with an "evangelical" bishop taking over his church from Wednesday to the following Sunday evening. The aim of the visit was to raise the profile of the church in the neighbouring schools and organisations. The team numbered eighteen in all with some very gifted people among it. The theme was "To have and to hold" with a strong emphasis upon the marriage bond. Terry later said that the mission was a turning point in the life of the church and a real strength to his ministry.

I carried on these outreach missions until we left Bath and Wells but was so encouraged by their success that later they became a feature of my ministry in the diocese of Canterbury.

The experience of that period, sharing deeply with Terry and his colleagues in those isolated parishes in that part of the diocese, made me acutely aware of the problems that many clergy face today and the inadequacy of the oversight that bishops and archdeacons are able to give. As a flat organisation, with no middle management to give direction and leadership, it is impressive that so many clergy do manage to lead struggling parishes with dignity and strength. I made it my vow to pay attention to this deficiency and to do all in my power to address it.

As a diocese, Bath and Wells is predominantly rural but it has some strong churches in places like Taunton, Bath, Glastonbury and Wells. In Bath, the central church is, of course, Bath Abbey. An impressive building, the abbey was the second most important church after Wells Cathedral in the diocese. Shortly before I took up office as bishop Eileen and I had had supper with Bishop Mervyn Stockwood, the retired Bishop of Southwark. During coffee, Mervyn took us to the main window, overlooking Bath, and drawing back the curtains to show the flood-lit abbey he said in his dramatic way: "See the abbey? That is the only light to come from the abbey these days!" We were then told of the decline of the abbey under the present rector, Geoffrey Lester, now in his twenty-sixth year. "If only Geoffrey had left after twenty years," Mervyn complained, "we would be talking of a highly successful ministry of preaching and service. But now, it is all decline and death." I could not take that at face value but, on taking up my new post, I was anxious to meet Geoffrey who was as near a recluse as any clergyman can get, and there were enough complaints made about him to fill several notebooks. However, the real story was of a spirited preaching ministry for twenty years until a broken marriage and illness cut short Geoffrey's fine work. It was not long before Eileen and I met him on our rounds to meet all the clergy. On entering his study, his first words were: "So, Bishop, you are here to tell me it is time to leave! That's right, isn't it?" The only way to play that was by not arguing but simply replying in a friendly Christian way. He was an older man, reduced by circumstances and robbed of his health; it was a moment that deserved sympathy and compassion and I replied, "No, Geoffrey, this is not the time to focus on leaving. You will know when that time comes and I will be here to assist you then." I continued, "We are here to meet fellow clergy and to hear of your ministry. Tell us about the abbey and your long ministry here."

It was actually a wonderful meeting and we were moved by the way Geoffrey spoke of his work in the glorious and historic Abbey building. Trust was built up between us in that first meeting, so I was not surprised when, some months later, he booked a meeting with me and his first words were, "Bishop, the time has come..." He left with dignity and praise for his great ministry, allowing a much younger man to take over.

We were tremendously sad to leave Bath and Wells after only two and a half years in the wonderful county of Somerset. There was a certain irony in the fact that it was in the middle of a mission I was leading in the deanery of Radstock that the invitation from the Prime Minister arrived. I had no idea that others felt that I could be a worthy Archbishop of Canterbury and I knew that I was very inexperienced. But the call came and, even though Eileen and I were far from prepared, we were willing. As we had never refused the Church's calling to serve, our faces turned towards Canterbury.

3

The Magnificence of Leadership

I am among you as one who serves.

Jesus of Nazareth

In my penultimate year as Archbishop four coordinated attacks from the Islamic group, Al-Qaeda, stunned the United States and the rest of the world with sophisticated assaults on the heartland of America. Two planes targeted the World Trade Centre, another the Pentagon, and the fourth, intended for Washington, was thwarted by passengers and crashed into a field in Pennsylvania. Some three thousand people died in that attack on the United States. However, it was not the number of victims that dismayed the intelligence services. It was the realisation that a new type of war had begun, this time by powerful Islamist groups which had resources and technological prowess to take the war to America. President George W. Bush labelled it a "war against terror".

September 11th, or 9/11, led indirectly to a change in my ministry and future work. A few days after 9/11, I preached at a national service in St Paul's to a largely young American congregation with Her Majesty as principal worshipper. It was a wonderful gesture by the Government and Church to the American people. Together, following the service, the Queen and I walked out on to the steps of St Paul's to mingle among the thousands of young Americans as, far from home, they sought hope in the power of the Christian message.

As a result of that terrible event I was invited, along with a number of other faith leaders, to take part in the World Economic Forum in January 2002. The World Economic Forum, founded by Dr Klaus Schwab, is a business organisation that gathers thousands of leaders annually at Davos in Switzerland for discussion, team building and networking. From modest beginnings it has become one of the most effective and important international meeting points. But Klaus Schwab and his senior team decided that the proper place for that particular World Economic Forum meeting, immediately after 9/11, was not Davos but New York. Representatives of the Pope were Cardinal Jean Tauran and Cardinal Theodore McCarrick; His All-Holiness the Metropolitan Patriarch of Constantinople was present on behalf of the Orthodox Churches; Sheikh Badawi and several imams; Chief Rabbi Dr Jonathan Sacks; Rabbi David Rosen and other faith leaders had been invited. With 9/11 so vivid in our memory it was an emotional as well as an amazing gathering of politicians, business, social entrepreneurs, with faith leaders. It brought home to many there the power of faith for evil as well as good, and gave those of us rooted in faith communities a deep desire to decry the appalling evil of those who use religion for political ends. Those four days in the luxury of the Waldorf-Astoria were an education in the sophistication of the world of big business – its opulence, thoroughness and focus. They also brought me into contact with some of the sharpest minds and personalities of the world. That brief exposure then took a surprising turn when Klaus Schwab, following my retirement from office at the end of 2002, invited me to join the Foundation Board of the WEF and to be the Coordinator of faith leaders. This then led me to regular meetings in Geneva with the Foundation Board, listening to their concerns and seeking to understand the breadth and depth of their responsibilities. These meetings of the Board, together with regular visits to the Headquarters of the WEF at Coligny, Switzerland, provided me with insights into a fundamental question: "What makes a great leader? What lessons can Christian leadership learn from secular examples of outstanding leadership?"

The World Economic Forum had been founded by Karl Schwab in 1971 when he was just thirty-three years of age. Although an engineer by profession he was already aware that companies were mainly interested in serving their shareholders. This was a total mistake in Schwab's opinion. Businesses, for Schwab, were there for their social capital as well as for making profits. Your clients, argued Schwab, were just as important as your shareholders. After an uncertain start, the Forum gradually caught the imagination and eventually the support of many businesses, and has since become the world's foremost public platform for private and public cooperation. Driven by Schwab's energy and foresight, the WEF has become a catalyst for change and all kinds of partnerships – including that of engagement with religious communities.

The Foundation Board was and remains a significant body of close friends and leading business and public figures with whom Karl could share his thinking and, in turn, receive from them advice and counsel. It was a rare privilege for a former Archbishop of Canterbury to be consulted in this way, but I knew there was much I could learn from this body. On the Board when I was welcomed were people from all walks of life with business people dominating. There were men and women of the calibre of Michael Dell, founder of Dell Computers; Queen Rania of Jordan; Larry Summers, President of Harvard; Ernesto Zedillo, former President of Mexico and Professor of International Economics and Politics at the University of Yale; Oscar Luigi Scalfaro, former President of Italy; Rajat Gupta, CEO of McKinsey; Orit Gadiesh, Chair of Bain and Co; and others.

The regular meetings of the Foundation Board offered many moments of discussion with individuals. If there was one notion that was quickly dismissed from my mind, it was that secular leadership at this senior level, where people were earning millions of dollars, was a piece of cake. There was no mistaking the tension, the worry of business, the extremely long hours and the sense of obligation to customers and to their boards. Rajat Gupta, the first foreign-born CEO of McKinsey, spoke openly about the stress of management and his awareness that his post was dependent upon success: "It could all come to an end pretty quickly," he said. Sadly, it did for him when in 2012 he was convicted of securities fraud and sentenced to two years in a penal establishment. Very oddly, one thing I remember him repeating were the words of his wife who warned him on several occasions that "you are too trusting and you think that everyone will be nice to you. Financial people are different from consultants. They'll eat you for lunch." But not everyone in business at the highest level ends up in jail and very few run such risks that imperil their careers.

It was at one of the meetings that Klaus Schwab offered his thinking on leadership and said that great leadership comes down to four factors: brains, soul, heart and good nerves. "As a leader you need to be professional and know what you are doing. That is brains. Your soul gives you direction; it is a compass and a vision. Your heart brings passion and compassion. Good nerves means composure in the face of critical crisis and the ability to remain calm."

I was struck by this description which matched my experience of leadership in a complex and historically confused body such as the Church of England. Breaking down those four elements one can see that each has a crucial role to play and none should trump the others. Brains refer to an intelligent grasp of the post and one's ability to lead an organisation. If you are not on top of the game, then you will be led, not lead. It means reflection on the task you are given to accomplish and being abreast of current thinking in your area of business. There has to be sufficient intellectual vision and ability that enables the person in charge to lead a team of motivated people. I was aware of the, no doubt fictitious, story of an army cadet whose CV included the words: "Men will only want to follow this officer from a sense of curiosity."

Klaus Schwab's take on "soul" interested me. He meant by "soul" an unwavering commitment to the values of the institution and attention to individuals: "Leaders should lead by compassion and not by radar." That is to say, you must be close enough to those you serve that you never run the risk of being out of touch. I saw an example of this when Nelson Mandela attended the World Economic Forum. Nelson was present at a small informal meeting of leaders when, looking at his watch, he suddenly asked someone if he could borrow a phone for a moment or two. He made a short call to South Africa, returned the phone and explained that when he had been released from prison in 1990, after having been absent for twenty-seven long years from his family, he vowed that he would phone one of his family every day at a certain time, to express his love and care for them. That attention to others was one of the special characteristics of Mandela whom Schwab said "was a leader who inspired by magnanimity, fortitude and dignity in the face of oppression".

Heart, according to Klaus Schwab, referred to that element of sensitivity and care which outstanding leaders possess. We might call it "feelings" which for Schwab meant knowing intuitively what the team was thinking and reading the mood of key leaders. For Schwab this did not mean knowing the entire story because he felt that great leaders never micro-managed. You must trust your colleagues and pay attention to their advice but there were times when you had to let go in order for proper decisions to be made. I was impressed by the way these top figures knew their intimate teams and took care of them.

Good nerves was Klaus Schwab's final point and was the conclusion he had reached after a survey of dozens of senior business people. How do people in major organisations cope with failure and crisis? For Schwab, effective leaders could face problems with equanimity and calmness, "with unwavering will even in the face of critical crisis." He went on to say, "Leaders must be bold and able to move toward their vision, even with incomplete information or risky odds."

There was, however, one other aspect of effective leadership which

I saw in Dr Schwab himself and that is an element of "ruthlessness" which, in his case, meant keeping to agreed plans and not allowing emotion or last minute hesitations to overthrow decisions made. In goal-setting at the Forum there was usually a time limit on any project , typically three years. Unless a particular module was doing extremely well, the Forum would expect to close it down when the time was reached. I myself became a victim of this when I was asked to co-chair the Council of 100. I was allowed four years and then the guillotine came down. No doubt Klaus had his reasons, but he never discussed them with me and, sadly, a successful project on mapping dialogue throughout the religious world never saw the light of day. Klaus knew I was disappointed but he handled the disagreement very professionally.

However, it is impossible to pin leadership down to a few points that, if followed, anyone can be an effective leader. It never works like that and so much depends upon circumstances, gifts, inclinations and nerve. Christian leadership is not greatly different except that Christians have a relationship with the greatest leader of all, and his example should be the stimulus for Christian people especially.

But what about the opposite – when leaders fail?

I have already mentioned the imprisonment of Rajat Gupta, former CEO of McKinsey & Co. This shocked the Board and, in the fringes of our meetings, I had several conversations concerning failure in leadership. I found a very refreshing attitude towards failure. In my own experience it had, on the whole, been a positive factor in that it drove me on to overcome handicaps. However, I had to admit as well that for most of my working life I had rather regarded it also as shameful. This was certainly not the attitude of these secular and successful figures. My attitude changed as a result. Coming into a somewhat elitist Church from a working-class background and having failed the eleven-plus, it was an encouragement to realise that failure is of little importance in the advancement of a career. I recall, on returning from doing my National Service, aged twenty, meeting a slightly older man, an ordinand, at a church meeting. On hearing that I, from a working-class background, was exploring ordination his contemptuous reply was: "Forget it, you'll never make it!" I never met him again but, rather than putting me off, his remark drove me to challenge his elitist assumptions. Failure is only failure when we give up the fight and yield to the expectations of others.

Naturally, no one in life has total success. We all fail at some point or another and Winston Churchill is perhaps the most successful failure ever. It was not a complete surprise then to find that my colleagues on the Foundation Board viewed failure as a very natural factor in all careers. It was, according to Ernesto Zedillo, former President of Mexico, a recurring factor in business life where success was a daily struggle against the uncertainties of the market and in competition against rivals. Where you were born, what schools and universities you attended – such factors played little role in their world of work. What mattered was your vision for your life's work, the business you represented, and your personal integrity in your leadership role. Larry Summers, the then President of Harvard University, was a case in point. Success and failure featured in equal measure throughout an eventful career. He was a very engaging man to talk with, and he made no secret of his strong views on the environment, elitism and the centrality of business ethics. He was not afraid to speak out on controversial matters and not prepared to back down, even if the majority were against him. Indeed, his view on gender equality led to his resignation as President of Harvard. It was a sad reminder that, when at the zenith of one's career, a simple error of judgment may bring all crashing down. In his case it was his decision to accept an invitation to give a talk at a lunch in January 2005 with his reflections on why many women are under-represented in "tenured positions in science and technology at top universities and research institutions". He began his address by saying that he was entirely positive towards women reaching the very top in science, and that his remarks were meant to provoke. He asserted that in the special case of science and engineering there are issues of intrinsic aptitude, and particularly of the variability of aptitude, and that these considerations are reinforced by what are, in fact, lesser factors involving socialisation and "continuing discrimination". This was picked up later as implying that women lack aptitude.   He ended by concluding, "I would like nothing better than to be proved wrong but these are my observations." He went on to offer thoughts on remedying the shortage of women in high-end science.

Summers spoke later at a meeting of the Foundation Board about his shock at the uproar that followed. That lunchtime talk had drawn accusations of sexism and careless scholarship. Within a year Larry Summers' career at Harvard was over, and a potential post of Treasury Secretary in the Obama administration was never to materialise. And yet, as Sharon Sandberg, Summers' assistant at Harvard, remarked:

> Larry has been a true advocate for women through his career. What few seemed to realise is that the reason he was giving the talk in the first place was that he cared enough about women's careers, and their trajectory in the fields of math and science, to analyse the issues and talk about what was going wrong.

Where did Summers transgress? It was certainly not in the area of inadequate research or scholarship, but it was possible that Summers was guilty of misreading the "zeitgeist" of the age and, at that particular time in America, it was the underlying belief that nothing separated male and female abilities other than discrimination, unfairness and prejudice. Summers' "sin" was to examine issues that were considered ultra vires. For Professor Steven Pinker, also on the Faculty of Harvard, Summers' talk was clearly within the pale of legitimate scholarship. "Good grief," he added, "there's certainly enough evidence for his hypothesis to be taken seriously. That's the difference between a university and a madrassa." I was glad to know that later, when all the fuss had subsided, Barack Obama stood by Summers and appointed him Director of the National Economic Council.

There are many benefits from nearly sixty years of Christian leadership, because it has given me insight into great personalities in the world and Church, and enabled me to marvel at our capacity for greatness and failure.

Leadership, however, is never exercised in a vacuum – the context is crucial. The leaders on the Board of the World Economic Forum exercised theirs in business, where little regard is given to tradition unless it sells, and where antiquity is regarded with contempt unless it is profitable.

My secular colleagues were amazed at the business approach of the Church of England. From their point of view, a CEO (Archbishop) who had forty-two separate and independent units (dioceses), each with its own separate business plan, was in charge of a business doomed to fail. I could not disagree with that. My experience of the Church of England was one of frustration at our inability to agree on what message to present, and our apparent contentment with mediocrity. Chairing the House of Bishops meetings was not something that I and other archbishops enjoyed. It was not that our bishop-colleagues were difficult people – they were not; they were serious, sincere and godly. It was a privilege to work with them. But the independent structures of the Church meant that each bishop was autonomous – an archbishop could only intervene when there was a major crisis. This was not conducive to creating policies on mission, evangelism and service. Evidence was stark that, measured by statistics, churches throughout the land were failing. All of the ways in which we measure growth – baptisms, confirmations, church attendance – were going in the wrong direction. Furthermore, it has been abundantly clear for some decades that church membership is no longer based upon family identification with a particular denomination, but is rather more loosely predicated on social factors such as the type of church service or the character of the minister. That break with family tradition is a very significant factor.

However, there was never an honest and open discussion at House of Bishops meetings about how we might create a policy of growth for the Church – how we might harness the rich national body of hundreds of churches to become a spiritual home for the nation once more. Sadly, to this day there is not one diocese which can be said to be an effective body reaching out with a clear and convincing Christian message. This will be denied because dioceses still think they are faithful. But the word I am highlighting is "effectiveness" not "faithfulness". The bleak conclusion is of episcopal failure which, as a member of that body for fourteen years, I shared.

My personal instincts, however, were to find ways of putting evangelism at the heart of being a bishop. I wrote in the previous chapter of my practice as Bishop of Bath and Wells to lead missions in the diocese with a lay team of musicians and actors. We would visit deaneries and parishes from a Wednesday to the following Sunday evening and share in the ministry of that parish or deanery. These were marvellous times of outreach and showed time and again how much this ministry was welcomed by the wider community. I continued this ministry in the diocese of Canterbury as Archbishop and saw again how much it helped to encourage the local church in its role within its parish, and how it also helped to break down the myth that the Christian faith had nothing to say about the "real" world. Sadly, few other bishops have followed this lead or have broken away from traditional roles of episcopal ministry. Candidly, I believe the fundamental reason is that few bishops have had any experience of growth in their formation as priests, and therefore have little concept of what it means to make disciples. I am not confident that this will ever be addressed.

With so little guidance from the "top", most clergy in their parishes have to plough a lonely furrow without support from their bishops – principally, as I have observed, because those in leadership have had no real experience of successful growth in ministry. Occasional reports like *Towards the Conversion of England* by William Temple in 1945 and more recently *Set My People Free* (2015) have not changed the mind-set or the will of the Church of England. Yet, in spite of this serious issue, my experience was that the Church was filled with many men and women of great ability, intellect and personality from whom I learned a lot.

In 1990 I was invited by Margaret Thatcher to become Archbishop of Canterbury. That totally unexpected and staggering invitation brought with it a deep worry for me because the other name in the frame was undoubtedly John Habgood, the formidable Archbishop of York. He had been my bishop when I was vicar of St Nic's Durham. In some ways he was a terrifying and aloof man, given to long silences, and was not known for his sense of humour. Eileen found him a difficult man as a dinner companion and many had stories to tell of his stern and stiff manner. He would have had every reason to feel hurt by a much younger and less experienced man being put ahead of him. If he did, he never showed it. The awkwardness that others complained about I never found. This may have been because, when I was parish priest of St Nic's Durham, I had had a car crash while visiting the prison and no one could have been kinder or more helpful afterwards than John Habgood. Although I could never claim that we became hand in glove, we worked together well. The ordination of women as priests was a case in point. John knew that I was keen to see this become law – an aspiration that he shared – and when it came to the debate in General Synod, it was John who suggested that I gave the main address leading the argument for the Ordination of Women and that he would keep his powder dry, because it was necessary for one of us to spend time listening to those who were opposed and to help them pastorally. I admired his intellectual gifts and the wisdom and patience that flowed from them.

A real test of our partnership came in 1994 when the *Financial Times* revealed that mismanagement at the Church Commissioners had led to the loss of nearly £800 million. An investigation later concluded that there was no criminal involvement, but it brought home the dire consequences when financial control was separated from the leadership of the Church. It was necessary to bring together the work of the Commissioners with that of the Church and that was done under the aegis of a new body named the Archbishops' Council. Frank Field MP, on the Board of the Church Commissioners, was someone who helped to make this a reality.

Whilst the Archbishops' Council is far from perfect, it has brought together the various limbs of the Church and made it a working body.

Thoroughness is an element of leadership and John possessed this in abundance. Sadly, in late retirement he became a victim of Alzheimer's and the Church lost a brilliant mind.

My fruitful partnership with John Habgood continued with his successor Archbishop David Hope who in 1995 moved from the challenging diocese of London to take up the demands of the northern province. Whereas John was a reserved and shy man, David was very personable, warm and pastorally able. David and I were at different ends of the classical Anglican churchmanship ladder but there was an affinity of minds because the element that binds evangelicals and Catholics together is a deep love of God in Christ. Indeed, the rivalry and bitterness that churchmanship used to create is largely a thing of the past. The Church is beginning to value the strengths of our splintered past. From David I learned the importance of giving time to individuals and following them up afterwards. David never dropped people or forgot their needs. This was accompanied by a delightful Yorkshire sense of humour. When, much later, we were both unfairly and wrongly accused of "colluding" with clergy who were sexual abusers, we were able to support each other at a time when it seemed that the hierarchy of the Church had disowned us.

In the north of England one of the real characters on the House of Bishops bench was Bishop David Jenkins. David and I had been colleagues when I was Principal of Trinity and he was Chair of the CNAA (Council for National Academic Awards). David was an outstanding academic and a first-class speaker, with an inclination for mischief. That he was appointed Bishop of Durham in 1984 surprised very few people, but I was not the least surprised when his addresses began to disturb the faithful and delight the media. He cast doubt on the Virgin Birth and dismayed orthodox Christians with his widely quoted statement that the resurrection of Christ was just a conjuring trick with bones. In fact, he had said that the resurrection of Christ was "not" just a conjuring trick with bones, but the phrase stuck and became folk lore.

Before becoming bishop, David's world had been academia where raising difficult questions was expected. As bishop he continued this habit and enjoyed the attention. He loved the publicity that he aroused but he was certainly not as liberal and unbelieving as the media made out. He added much needed fun to the House of Bishops meetings and made a serious contribution to the intellectual depth of the Church. It was regrettable that he became known for his doubts and not for his well-established beliefs. Sadly, from my perspective, David was never a team player. He loved to be a "prima donna" enjoying the limelight alone. Effective leadership is a gift to be shared and owned by others.

Bishop David Sheppard, the Bishop of Liverpool, was another outstanding Christian leader. I had known David when he was leader of the Mayflower Family Centre in the East End of London. Of course, David Sheppard was internationally famous as a distinguished cricketer. Within the Church he was beginning in the 1960s to make waves as an up and coming evangelical leader. He began his ministry as curate at St Mary's Islington where, ten years later, I was to follow in that same position.

There were two sides to David Sheppard; he never let go his evangelical principles but his gospel became increasingly social and political as his ministry widened. His book, *Bias to the Poor*, was as much a protest against a divided society, in which the poor were victims, as it was a statement of belief.[8] In his own words, "The gospel is both about changing people from inside out and changing the course of events to set people free."

On retirement, David was offered a peerage on the Labour benches of the House of Lords. I must admit that I was sad to see the evangelical side of his faith declining in importance, but there was no doubt that David's commitment to ordinary people was recognised and admired. He was one of the key writers of the influential *Faith in the City* report published in 1985.

But there was another side to David which was very influential ecumenically. During his twenty-two years as Bishop of Liverpool, a strong friendship developed between David Sheppard and Derek Worlock, the Roman Catholic Archbishop of Liverpool. David lost some former evangelical friends as Derek and he worked together, but I was among the many who saw this as a very prophetic partnership which would bless both of our churches. I attended David's funeral in his magnificent cathedral where one of the speakers referred to him as a "catholic evangelical". From David I learned the importance of keeping to your principles and not fearing criticism, whether it came from the world or from the Church.

My life as priest, bishop and archbishop occurred at a time when the voices of women were subdued. Yet I had never been in doubt about the power of women, of which there are many examples in history and secular society. As I mentioned in Chapter 1 my thinking on the role of women in the church was changed through working with Doreen Bergernie at St Mary's Islington. "Lady workers" was the official term for laywomen at the time who served in the Church. Their job essentially was limited to working with women and children. Such workers had no liturgical role and, in fact, a more lowly position could not be imagined. Yet it was impossible to suppress Doreen. The many gifts of this remarkably clever woman became apparent. After all, she had trained as an actress through RADA and had had several roles on stage. Like us male curates, she felt strongly called to serve Christ in some role and she was the only woman on an all-male staff of one vicar and four young men. The irony was that she was far more experienced than the curates and, truly, a first-rate speaker. Working so closely with Doreen brought home to me the stupidity of Samuel Johnson's statement: "Sir, a woman's preaching is like a dog's walking on his hind legs. It is not done well; but you are surprised to find it done at all." What nonsense is that? Alas, Doreen's struggle with breast cancer left her little time to exercise the role of a priest in the Church of God, as she died a few days after I had ordained her in 1995, but her legacy was in my determination – shared by the majority in the House of Bishops – to get the legislation through Synod and into law. We are now blessed to have many gifted women in the ordained ministry as clergy and bishops.

Abroad, there were so many outstanding leaders that I admired. Desmond Tutu stands out by his awesome courage and terrific sense of humour. But what few knew was that those outward gifts were supported by a life of prayer and a deep Anglo-Catholic spirituality. I recall those times when staying at Bishopscourt in Cape Town we would say the Daily Office in his chapel, early in the morning, before his relentless activities commenced. If Nelson Mandela was the political face and voice of the struggle for black people in South Africa, Desmond was its spiritual and Christian face. His mischievous sense of humour, allied to African dance, gave a human quality to his demands for equality.

A far less known African leader was David Gitari, Archbishop of Kenya. I was particularly fond of David who, like me, was born into a poor home but blessed with Christian parents. In the three visits I paid to Kenya I saw the uncompromising leadership of David Gitari and how he stood out against corruption and political imperialism. The pressure on many churches in Africa – as well as elsewhere – is to adapt passively to the affairs of the state and refrain from comment on political issues. David was often under attack for challenging this understanding. President arap Moi said on many occasions that "the Church has a duty to speak out against corruption and other evils". But, as David pointed out regularly, "every time a church leader speaks openly against corruption and injustice, he is told to leave politics to the politicians!" I remember a particularly tense moment when, on a visit to Nairobi, I was invited by President arap Moi to attend the National Parade and sit alongside David Gitari. David spoke first and warned the nation of the dangers of corruption and, from the Bible, the way it destroys a people. I could see on the President's face his growing anger as David's fearless barbs struck home. Then, at the President's invitation, I spoke. I had decided beforehand that I would speak more on lessons the UK had learned from failure to serve the poor, as well as emphasising David's argument about impartiality. Then the President spoke, and he began by turning on me and saying, "We have no need for lessons from the UK and the West. If there are any seeds of injustice in Kenya, then let it be known that your country has sown them!" This was greeted with great applause but then, very courteously, the President thanked me for visiting his country. Afterwards at the reception and in our private meeting, with David present, no one could have been more affable and welcoming. It made me realise that it is not only celebrities who play to the crowd; politicians too have often contradictory messages that they hold together. David went on to be a consistent friend to politicians, unswerving in his commitment to justice and truth, and never giving in to the offer of bribes that would have ended his prophetic ministry. David's example of a holy commitment to his nation arose from his deeper commitment to the scriptures. Such amazing leadership.

Another outstanding but much younger leader is Canon Andrew White. I first met him at Lambeth Palace when I hosted a reception for the Council of Christians and Jews (CCJ). Andrew at that time was Vicar of Balham Hill but I could see he was deeply committed to peace in the Middle East. I was not only attracted by his knowledge of key Muslim and Jewish leaders in Israel but also by his effective collaboration with people like Shimon Peres, President of Israel, and Rabbi Michael Melchior, who was then in the Israeli Government. Eventually, and a few years later, Andrew was a natural choice for the post of Director of the International Centre for Reconciliation of Coventry Cathedral, with Justin Welby as one of his assistants. With extraordinary vision and energy Andrew made an instant impact by bringing together religious leaders. His friendship with Rabbi Michael Melchior and Sheikh Talal Al-Sider was a visible sign of friendship amongst different faiths. Sheikh Talal Al-Sider was a founder of the Palestine Liberation Organisation (PLO) but as time went on had many regrets about how the movement became murderous. It was Andrew who, following 9/11, approached me to ask if I could broker a meeting between the religious leaders of the Middle East. This was followed by a phone call from Shimon Peres asking for the same thing and promising resources from the Israeli

Government. The British Government was equally supportive, as was the Egyptian Government. The irony was that we were unable to meet in Israel but hospitality given by President Mubarak of Egypt led to a historic meeting of Middle East religious leaders in Alexandria, whence the document *The Alexandria Declaration* was the result. It was the most demanding meeting I have ever chaired but one of the most satisfying. In short, the Declaration argued for peace among the religions and committed the main religions to work together for the good of our communities. This agreement led to other and similar statements in Iraq and northern Nigeria. It was Andrew's drive, vision and determination that saw these agreements succeed, against a background of his own serious and debilitating illness.

Another outstanding leader with natural gifts and a warm outgoing personality is Dr Patrick Sookhdeo, the International Director of Barnabas Fund. It is among the many sadnesses of my life that I only met Patrick in retirement. He is one of the most remarkable, yet overlooked leaders in the Anglican Communion. (Patrick resigned from the Church of England a decade ago because of the harassment, abuse and racism that he received.) Born into a Muslim family in South America, Patrick moved with his family in 1959 to the UK and became a Christian as a student in London. The holder of three doctorates, Patrick saw his vocation initially in teaching and building up congregations in the East End of London. He quickly became a popular speaker encouraging and developing new ministries. Together with Rosemary, his wife, Patrick founded In Contact Ministries, a ministry of church planting, and then went on to found and direct the Institute for the Study of Islam and Christianity. He is a widely acknowledged authority on Islam and security issues and has acted as a consultant and adviser to government, business and the media, especially on contemporary Islamist terrorism, and has lectured at various conferences on security and terrorism in the UK and in the USA (for both the US military and the FBI). He has briefed senior military commanders both in the UK and in the USA including Special Operations and Southern

Command. He has been involved in pre-deployment training for UK armed forces and served as an adviser to Permanent Joint Headquarters UK and as an adviser to the FBI. He has moderated the annual Counter-Terrorism Symposium at the Defence Academy of the UK. Patrick and his wife Rosemary founded Barnabas Fund, an aid agency which assists persecuted Christians in more than 80 countries around the world. What stands out in Patrick's style of leadership is the capacity to motivate and inspire others.

Leadership, therefore, is a mysterious quality that we all possess in some shape or form but some have in abundance. As I see it now, among the intangible links that unite the different worlds of business, politics and faith is the willingness of the leader to go out on a limb and take risks. This factor is clearly there in the teaching of Jesus where, in Luke 14, the Lord speaks of a king contemplating war against an enemy who has double the number of soldiers. The message is clear: boldness is all very well but be sensible, think it through. But, in verse 33 comes the fundamental challenge: "In the same way, those of you who are not able to give up everything, cannot be my disciples." And it is in this radical understanding of discipleship that the true character of leadership is found – the capacity to give yourself wholeheartedly to the cause.

As Klaus Schwab put it, the mysterious quality of leadership will require that mixture of brain, soul, heart and nerve; but essentially leadership is that ability to get things done, and if you do not get things done – you are not a leader.

4

Dangerous, Decadent and Divisive?

Men never do evil so completely and cheerfully as when they do it from religious conviction.

Blaise Pascal

From the perspective of the 2020s it is incredible to think that, until the final decade of the twentieth century, faiths other than Christianity were hardly visible in the United Kingdom. When I became Archbishop in 1991, work with other faiths was not a major item on my agenda. There were regular meetings of the Inter-Faith Network of which I was a President, and these meetings were always enjoyable and usually associated with exotic food. I always found working with Hindus, Buddhists, Sikhs and other non-Abrahamic faiths pleasurable and interesting. The unspoken agreement was that our meetings were all about living together in harmony.

From a Christian perspective, Judaism was a more important priority and Jews were a visible and important group in Britain, in spite of their small numbers. Indeed, on my appointment I found that I was one of the Presidents of the Council of Christians and

Jews – founded in 1942 by Chief Rabbi Joseph Hertz and William Temple, Archbishop of Canterbury. It was an important group to be part of.

Almost immediately after I was appointed Archbishop, Rabbi Jonathan Sacks was selected to be Chief Rabbi and straight away we became good friends. A uniting factor was our love of Arsenal FC and one of our earliest meetings was at Highbury when Arsenal played its arch-rival Manchester United. The club were keen to welcome us, and before the game we walked on to the hallowed turf to present a cheque to a charity. This was followed by a game in which Arsenal was outclassed by Manchester United who won 5-2. The CEO of Arsenal was not impressed: "Archbishop and Chief Rabbi," he said, "you are always welcome here, but if we play like that whenever you turn up, don't come too often!"

Jonathan's warm personality, to say nothing of his considerable scholarship and the outstanding books he churned out regularly, established a strong friendship between us. For myself and many Christians, Judaism could not be seen as a strange and hostile religion, as it had been for many Christians in the past. The roots of Christianity lie in the faith of Israel and the Hebrew scriptures. Indeed, at every act of worship in the Anglican Communion we join with Jews the world over in our devotion to the Psalms and its spirituality. How can any Christian ever forget that Jesus himself was a loyal Jew and cannot be understood apart from it? As a young Christian growing up after the war, the shocking pictures of the concentration camps brought home to me the suffering of the Jewish people. And yet in the horrors of the Holocaust lies the problem of "theodicy"; how could a good and great Yahweh allow his people to die in such horror and degradation? Here the abandonment of Israel and the abandonment of Jesus can be seen as one: "My God, my God, why have you forsaken me?" (Matthew 27:46) I saw Israel as the forsaken people who following that terrible war regained their ancient land and transformed a wilderness into a Garden of Eden. Truly Christianity is a child of Judaism.

Judaism, like Christianity, is not defined by the Orthodox

tradition. There are many different forms of Judaism of varying conformities to the world around and their own historic traditions: Liberal Judaism, United Synagogue, Movement for Reform Judaism, among others. Within the Reform tradition three outstanding rabbis were to become firm friends alongside Jonathan Sacks, the leader of Orthodox Jews. Rabbi Hugo Gryn came from a Holocaust family. His brother was gassed at Auschwitz. Hugo and his parents narrowly escaped. Hugo made a huge contribution to life in the United Kingdom and was a very popular speaker and broadcaster. Another well-known rabbi was Tony Bayfield, also highly respected and admired. A third, and much younger, rabbi was Dr Jonathan Romain, also a dynamic and lively communicator. It is quite remarkable that the relatively small number of rabbis in training are able to produce so many scholars of outstanding ability. My reflection on that issue led me to conclude that it was because of two significant factors. The first is the Jewish community's emphasis upon education, giving both boys and girls a firm civil education that could compete with the best in the secular world. The second reason for me was more important – the emphasis in Judaism on the "Word" (*davar*). Reading the Hebrew scriptures from infancy and studying the holy text gave to each student an awareness of reading as the entry to education and civilisation. The same thrust was there in Christianity in England in the growth of the Reformation churches in the sixteenth century, as the Bible was handed back to the people in the vernacular. Thereafter the Bible transformed the lives of many individuals and ultimately the nation.

A lay Jew of tremendous energy and ability was Sir Sigmund Sternberg, known widely as Sigi, who became a very significant figure in Britain and a personal friend. Sigi was born into a large and happy Jewish family in Budapest in 1921. As a teenager he watched with concern as Europe descended into totalitarianism, war and chaos. His family sought to protect him and he left his homeland in 1939 arriving in London to begin a new life. With his legendary energy and ability he soon became a successful businessman. His gratitude to Britain was great, and he never forgot the kindness of the British and their welcome to him. By 1965 Sigi's businesses were so extensive that he had sufficient resources to retire and give his attention to strengthening the ties between the Abrahamic faiths. Sigi was a man of faith but wore it lightly. A liberal Jew, he had little time for the food laws of strict Orthodoxy. However, whatever he lacked in religiosity he more than made up for by his awesome drive and determined will.

We became good friends and at Lambeth I hosted several dinners in his honour. Early on in my time as Archbishop he came to seek my backing and blessing for a new project. Although a great supporter of the Council of Christians and Jews he felt that the growing numbers of Muslims residing in the UK demanded a new kind of organisation.

It was here that I made a great mistake. I was so worried about the consequences of weakening the importance and strength of the CCJ that I felt that I could not publicly support what became known as the Three Faiths Forum, which was founded by Sir Sigi, Sheikh Zaki Badawi and the Rev Marcus Braybrooke, a good friend of mine. The Three Faiths Forum went on to be a major uniting force among the three major Abrahamic religions in the UK.

Sadly, throughout my time as Archbishop and afterwards in retirement, anti-Semitism continued to throw its long and dark shadow over society and affected relationships between Jewish and other faith communities. Even a superficial knowledge of English history can easily show that the cry "England has always welcomed the Jews" is a boast without substance. At times we have treated Jews shamefully. In 2016 Dr Sacks put the problem tersely: "In the Middle Ages, Jews were hated for their religion. In the nineteenth century they were hated for their race. Today, they are hated for their nation state." In January 2015 the Parliament of the United Kingdom addressed the issue with the conclusion that:

> Broadly, it is our view that any remark, insult or act the purpose or effect of which is to violate a Jewish person's dignity or create an intimidating, hostile,

degrading, humiliating or offensive environment for that person is antisemitic. This reflects the definition of harassment under the Race Relations Act 1976.

Prime Minister David Cameron welcomed the report on anti-Semitism with the comment that "Britain is proud to be a multi-ethnic, multi-faith democracy... While I am Prime Minister, I promise we will fight anti-Semitism with everything we have got." But rhetoric is one thing, reality is another. It is true that Britain remains a welcoming place for Jews and many Jews agree. David Hirsch, a prominent Jewish writer and activist, has said: "Jewish life in the UK is still rich and free. In spite of legitimate fear of terrorist attack ... Jews are not subjected to significant violence on the streets."[9] The same point was made by Jonathan Arkush, the then President of the Board of Deputies, who wrote:

> Britain is not an anti-semitic country. It is a broad-minded tolerant nation in which the Jewish community is not only accepted but appreciated for its immense contribution across almost every field imaginable. Yet anti-semitic attitudes stubbornly persist in a few dark corners, as they do virtually everywhere in the world.[10]

I almost choked on my toast when I read those last charitable words. In fact, David Cameron's vow was made against a background of turmoil in the Labour Party as that political strand – to which Jews had made profound contributions to over the years – was tearing itself apart over the issue of anti-Semitism. Jeremy Corbyn, its leader, appeared unable to drive from his party the ugly disease of Jew-hatred, as party members seemed to be queuing up to hurl abuse at Jewish people. In a lecture I gave to the Wiesenthal Foundation in New York under the title "Combatting History's Oldest Hate" I expressed my misgivings that the Labour Party was in possession of a death wish in its failure to eradicate the language, behaviour and attitudes reminiscent of 1930s Germany.

"All democratic political institutions," I said, "must express the highest expectations of equality, fairness and civility. That this is under threat in a prominent political party, where Jews have played and are playing significant and important roles, is a worrying sign of a society under threat." Sir Keir Starmer, who followed Corbyn as leader, has made great strides to get on top of the problem but anti-Semitism remains an ever present threat to liberal democracies in the West.

Before becoming Archbishop I was familiar with Judaism and had Jewish friends, but Islam for me was a subject read about in books. Apart from my period in the Royal Air Force in Egypt and Iraq, where I started to learn Arabic, I had had no contact at any level with Muslims. This was to change during the 1990s. Sheikh Zaki Badawi was Chief Imam at Regent's Park Mosque and, in the absence of a clear hierarchy in the Muslim faith, was effectively the spokesman for Islam in England. He greeted news of my appointment to Canterbury with some disparaging comments, fearing that my evangelical background would predispose me against Islam. So, within a few months of taking up office, I went out of my way to meet him. I think both of us were more than a little surprised to find that our misgivings were misplaced. I met, not a firebrand for Islam, but an intelligent, moderate man with a great sense of humour. He was reported to have said later that I was a reasonable chap also. Zaki always spoke with force and passion. The morning following the events of the World Trade Centre we were on BBC Radio 4's *Today* programme facing John Humphrys. Humphrys seemed keen to divide us and was clearly nonplussed that we were of one mind concerning terror and the use of violence by religions. Yes, there were differences in our approach in many respects, but on that issue we were agreed: our task was to assist our communities to live together in harmony and peace.

Sheikh Badawi was very concerned about the integration of Islam in the Western world. His constant worry was that Islam had no experience of living as minority communities in a largely secular Western civilisation and he spent a great deal of his time interpreting Islam to the West, and the West to the growing Muslim communities in the United Kingdom. Zaki passed away suddenly in 2006 and has left a gap in the religious world of the UK that no other leader from the Muslim faith has been able to fill.

The events of 9/11 changed everything. The dreadful attack on America led to an immediate backlash against American Muslims. The association of Islam with the most deadly terrorist attack in US history led to many ordinary American Muslims becoming victims of discrimination, hostility and violence. Despite Congress passing a resolution to stop scapegoating, mosques were attacked, some Muslims were injured and hate-crimes increased. The same happened in many other Western countries.

For myself, by now in retirement and the Co-ordinator of the World Economic Forum's religious arm, an unusual challenge came from an idea at the Foundation Board that there was a serious need for business people to understand the power of religion and its presence in the modern world. This was music to my ears because my encounter with colleagues at the World Economic Forum showed deep prejudice and woeful knowledge of all faiths. One meeting with a group of business people from the States and Europe led to a heated exchange where we were told that, despite its presence throughout the world, religion was not regarded as a positive binding force. The reasons given were threefold: religions were difficult, dangerous and divisive. Each of those descriptions was open to challenge and each illustrated, for me, the desperate need to find ways of building bridges.

Among the many qualities of Professor Klaus Schwab was his capacity to get things done and to move quickly with the resources of WEF behind him. A quick telephone conversation with him led to the idea of the "Council of 100" to bring faith and business together. It became my responsibility, together with Prince Turki bin Faisal Al Saud, to lead a body of one hundred leaders from five areas of life: religion, politics, business, art and journalism. Our task was to seek to bridge the gulf between the West and the Muslim world by three streams: dialogue, culture and action.

It was an exciting project and demanded firm leadership from myself and HE Prince Turki. I found the Prince a charming and sophisticated colleague. He was Ambassador to the United Kingdom and a popular figure among the Diplomatic Corps of the time. A very Westernised man, Prince Turki spoke the language of democracy, tolerance and the centrality of human rights but, in truth, it was in name only. Our C-100 meetings inevitably brought out the differences between the religions and there were several tense exchanges between the two of us, and between our Muslim colleagues and the non-Muslim participants. There was one explosive moment when he had made several comments about Saudi Arabia welcoming other religions. There was stunned and amazed silence. At once delegates began to point out that other religions were not welcome in his country, that Christianity and other non-Islamic faiths could not be practised there. He listened patiently and then explained that as Islam is the culmination of all faiths, it was simply a matter of all people following the Prophet of Islam. This was greeted as a silly effort to avoid the true offence that Islam gave in Saudi and, often, in other Muslim countries – namely, an arrogance that sprang from an unwillingness to engage. Sadly, Prince Turki lasted only fifteen months as Co-Leader because his country then wanted him to be Ambassador to the United States, so his sister, Princess Lolwah al-Faisal, became my colleague at C-100. Whereas her brother was outgoing and never lost for words, Princess Lolwah was quiet and left most of the chairing to me. But she was very keen to empower women and established strong relationships with several women on the Council. I detected in the Princess, and the group of Saudi women who accompanied her, a great desire to open up her country and faith to others. The dialogue at the Council was never easy and often tense.

During the lifetime of the Council two incidents occurred which led to major disagreements. The first was the uproar over the Danish cartoons and the offence they gave to Muslims. The Council came into its own as we grappled with the implications of cartoons mocking Muhammad, the Islamic prophet. It was not only that millions of Muslims objected to such a lack of respect, but also that Islam has a strong tradition of aniconism – the absence of material representation of religious figures. Indeed, for a brief moment in the eighth century Eastern Christianity took the same view. The crude depictions of Muhammad led to demonstrations around the world resulting in more than two hundred deaths and damage to church property.

The seniority of religious leaders at the C-100 meant that we were able to confer speedily and influence, down the line, many in our countries who were caught up in the protests. We were all agreed that the irresponsibility of the Danish paper, and the refusal of the Danish Government to meet with diplomatic representatives of Muslim countries, simply poured oil on burning waters. The Council was well equipped to handle the central issue of the "cartoon controversy" which was that of free speech. However, that it was a legitimate exercise of free speech was denied by Princess Lolwah and Muslims present. For them the central figure of their faith was under attack and post 9/11 this episode demonstrated the West's hostility to Islam. The Muslims had a point. Most people in the West fail to comprehend the importance for Muslims of the model of their prophet. Whilst Islam has consistently held to the full humanity of Muhammad he is seen as the very model of a human life – the ideal human. As founder of the faith Muhammad has a threefold role: prophet, warrior and statesman. As prophet, he received the message from Allah for a "new world order". As warrior, he was entrusted with force to make the message a reality. As statesman, he was given authority to maintain the message within human society. I am by no means justifying Muslim opposition to the cartoons but I am able to sympathise with and understand their anger and distress. The statement issued by the WEF expressed the Council's strong protest against those who used freedom of speech as a weapon against Islam, but also stressed the need to speak freely.

After my retirement, another matter affected me deeply. To my dismay and with Jewish leaders present, the General Synod of the

Church of England called for "divestment" from certain businesses working in Israel – which I believed was another example of the residual anti-Semitism that I referred to earlier. I was aware that such an action was done in good faith and was well intentioned by many. However, as I saw it, the effects of the call to oppose businesses working in Israel are not only to weaken that country materially but also indirectly to question the legitimacy of Israel and its right to self-defence. It represented the same distorted obsession with the actions of the state of Israel which we saw on the left of the Labour Party under Jeremy Corbyn. On that issue the Council of 100 was of one mind and was agreed that the call to weaken Israel by such actions was one-sided and wrong.

In both cases it is worth considering the law of unintended consequences. Applying this to the Danish cartoons, would the papers have printed the cartoons if they had known that many would lose their lives, churches be burnt to the ground and political damage result? I think not. And, in the case of the General Synod's call to "divest" from Israel, would the delegates have done so if they had known the consequences? Thankfully, Synod did later change its mind as it realised the lack of balance in its earlier reaction to Israel. My voice, and that of Canon Andrew White, were raised in protest against this badly thought-out strategy. The C-100 was a very helpful forum to raise such matters where politics and faith clashed.

The WEF's manner of working was never to allow ideas or projects to linger for ever and, as I have mentioned already, the C-100 received its marching orders after four years of working. Ironically, the closing down of the Council came just as we had finished a piece of work that had great potential. The project we had just completed was a mapping of all dialogues throughout the world. It represented a crucial step towards establishing good relations among the faiths and, similarly to *The Alexandria Declaration*, to reaching an agreement about violence in the name of religion. I was able to present this with a flourish to the Foundation Board. That evening Klaus and his wife took us to dinner and he explained that the C-100's work was now over. The WEF had moved on. It was a disappointing end to a very promising concept.

In 2005 I was totally unprepared for an explosion I caused internationally. I was accused of giving offence to Islam in a widely reported lecture given in Rome. I had spent a very agreeable four months at the Pontifical Gregorian University teaching a course at that prestigious and ancient school on ecumenical theology, as the McCarthy Visiting Professor. The course was endowed by Dr McCarthy, an American Catholic layman, and apart from the teaching load each week, the only other commitment was a lecture to culminate the visit. I chose to lecture on Islam and the title of the address was "Christianity and Islam: Collision or Convergence". I intended it to be hard-hitting but also fair and wide-ranging. I began by outlining the problem as I saw it:

> At the heart of our concern is Islam; a faith, a civilisation and a culture. A faith that is growing fast in every part of the world; a civilisation that has contributed greatly to the human family and still has much to offer; a culture, with a unique texture that appeals to millions. However, wherever we look, Islam seems to be embroiled in conflict with other faiths and other cultures. It is in opposition to practically every other world religion – to Judaism in the Middle East; to Christianity in the West, in Nigeria, and in the Middle East; to Hinduism in India; to Buddhism, especially since the destruction of the temples in Afghanistan. We are presented therefore with a huge puzzle concerning Islam. Why is it associated with violence throughout the world? Is extremism so ineluctably bound up with its faith that we are at last seeing its true character? Or could it be that a fight for the soul of Islam is going on that requires another great faith, Christianity, to support and encourage the vast majority of Muslims who resist this identification of their faith with terrorism?

I went on to address many of the challenges facing Muslims and in particular I observed that that there was surely a need for Islamic scholarship to be more open to examination and criticism. I observed that, in the first few centuries of the Islamic era, Islamic theologians sought to meet the challenge this implied, but over the past seven hundred years critical scholarship on the Quran has declined, leading to strong resistance to modernity. I admitted that it is sometimes very painful for the faithful when their sacred scriptures come under fierce examination and remarked, "Christianity and Judaism have had a long history of critical scholarship which, we must admit and acknowledge, has not been without its pain, but there have been great gains also." There was much else besides that I observed that was straight talking especially in connection with violence:

> A further challenge facing moderate Muslims is to resist strongly the taking over of Islam by radical activists and to express strongly, on behalf of the many millions of their co-religionists, their abhorrence of violence done in the name of Allah. We look to them to condemn suicide bombers and terrorists who use Islam as a weapon to destabilise and destroy innocent lives. Sadly, apart from a few courageous examples, very few Muslim leaders condemn, clearly and unconditionally, the evil of suicide bombers who kill innocent people.

Rather like Larry Summers in the last chapter I did not expect the wave of anger and condemnation that immediately followed the lecture. The following day in Rome I found myself in interview after interview, including BBC *Newsnight*, attempting to explain my concerns and approach. It was clear that my reasoned lecture was being interpreted in a way that I never intended, and the entire guts of my argument had been totally obscured by false interpretations that challenged my emphasis on convergence. As I explained to reporter after reporter, my entire relationship with Muslim leaders was based on friendship but also on frank talking. There was nothing in that address, I argued, that I had not said at least ten times in the past and always on the basis of being positive and constructive. I was astonished by the way that friends in the United Kingdom turned against me on the basis of the reporting. But within a few days the dust settled and, when people actually read the lecture as given, I was rewarded with apologies and explanations. It showed me the power and influence of the media, and how lazy journalists can damage relationships between faiths by misleading or, even worse, deliberately mischievous reporting.

The following year it was Pope Benedict's turn to feel the wrath of Muslims around the world, again illustrating the sensitivity of religious dialogue, when on September 12th 2006 he returned to Regensburg, where he had served as Professor of Theology, to give a lecture entitled "Faith, Reason and the University – Memory and Reflections". It was a careful and scholarly examination of the relations of faith to reason. The offending statement was a quotation of Emperor Manuel II, one of the last Christian rulers before the Fall of Constantinople, who had said: "Show me just what Muhammad brought that was new, and there you will find things only evil and inhuman, such as his command to spread by the sword the faith he preached." The Pope was comparing apparently contradictory passages from the Quran, one being that "there is no compulsion in religion" (Quran 2:256) and the other indicating that it is acceptable to spread the faith through violence. Even a casual reading of the lecture will show that it was never the Pope's intention to offend: he was simply arguing that spreading faith through violence is unreasonable. Although the Pope received much criticism from Muslims around the world from a superficial reading of the address, his attempt to show how faith untethered from reason leads to fanaticism and violence was sadly shown to be valid a few years later with the rise of Islamic State (IS, ISIS, ISIL, Daesh) and its aim of re-establishing a Caliphate.

In 2008 my successor as Archbishop of Canterbury, Rowan

Williams, was to receive similar critical treatment through a lecture he gave at the Royal Courts of Justice entitled: "Civil and Religious Law in England – a Religious Perspective". I have always been an admirer of Rowan's enviable scholarship and his erudite writings. However, on this matter I was deeply worried by his argument, and the way it would be used as Muslim propaganda. Addressing the sensitive subject of sharia law, and its centrality in Islam's faith and jurisprudence, Dr Williams argued that giving Islamic law official status in the UK would help achieve social cohesion because some Muslims did not relate to the British legal system. He said it was a "matter of fact" that sharia law was already being practised in Britain, and stated:

> It's not as if we're bringing in an alien and rival system; we already have in this country a number of situations in which the internal law of religious communities is recognised by the law of the land ... There is a place for finding what would be a constructive accommodation with some aspects of Muslim law as we already do with some kinds of aspects of other religious law.

The Archbishop's intention was sincere and was meant to be constructive but it was immediately met with fierce denunciations. No. 10 insisted that British law must be based on British values, and that sharia law should not be used as a justification for acting against national law. The Conservative Party spokesperson, Baroness Warsi, herself a Muslim, was equally clear: "The Archbishop's comments are unhelpful and may add to the confusion that already exists in our communities ... We must ensure that people of all backgrounds and religions are treated equally before the law."

I myself entered into the fray by recognising the positive aspects of my successor's nuanced lecture but arguing that no country can have two different and competing laws; sharia must be subservient to the law of the land. Whilst some Muslim groups rejoiced at the statements of the Archbishop, such was the almost universal condemnation that there were calls for him to resign. I was asked my opinion and said: "This is not a matter upon which Dr Williams should resign. He is a great leader in the Anglican Communion and has an important role to play in the Church."

In fact, the lecture was helpful in bringing a serious matter out into the open so that the general public could engage with a burning issue that affected Muslim women in particular. As a close associate of Baroness Cox, I was very concerned by the plight of Muslim women, married under sharia law and subject to its courts. She has drawn the House of Lords' attention to the reality of women living in Islamic marriages in Britain, not recognised by British law and lacking the rights that such recognition brings. There could be, she argues, as many as a hundred thousand women in this predicament. The debate on this continues and, supporting Baroness Cox, I am anxious to link Islamic marriage to civil marriage, so that Muslim women have the full protection of marital law afforded to them. Something similar to modern-day slavery is going on in some Muslim families in the United Kingdom.

The burning issue facing Britain today is whether or not Islamic values are compatible with the values of a Western democracy like the United Kingdom. At one level the answer could be put from the experiences of many Muslims living in our jostling communities: "Of course, why not? The evidence is all around us of many Muslims enjoying life and mixing well with other cultures." But there is also a more worrying side of the question. There are parts of our country where Muslim communities never engage with other cultures, and where triumphalistic and violent messages come from Salafist mosques. We must heed warning signs from our nearest neighbour, France, where the unrest and clash between the numerous Muslim communities and the general "laïque" population is dire. Our country, unlike France, has chosen not to rule on Islamic dress, whether it is hijab, niqab, or a simple scarf. We have taken the more sensible approach, disapproving the face being covered and tolerating the scarf which allows the face to be seen fully. The experience in France is that making this a matter of law has actually driven communities apart.

However, the UK cannot be complacent. A significant report in 2017, *Fear and Hope*, based on a Populus survey of over 4,000 people and billed as "one of the most comprehensive studies of English attitudes", found that attitudes towards Muslims and Islam had worsened. The survey showed that 25 per cent of English people believed that Islam is a dangerous religion and 52 per cent concluded that Islam is a threat to the West. Yet I know, when I look at the world through the eyes of Sheikh Zaki Badawi and many other Muslim leaders I have met, that this judgment is as false as it is dangerous. There are thousands of good Muslims who simply want to live their lives as faithful followers of their prophet, wherever they are in the world, and to make contributions to the places where they live.

Realism about religion today is a vital element of living together. As the great Kenneth Cragg once said: "Religion is as adept as politics in the art of self-justification." Whilst we must not judge Islam by the cruelty of IS or the rage of hurt people objecting to Danish cartoons, we have to recognise that obscurantism, ignorance and prejudice can be found everywhere. I find myself reminding Muslims again and again that "Islamophobia" does not mean "hatred" of Islam but "fear" of Islam and, sadly, that reality is still there. Strictly speaking, fear and hatred are two sides of the same coin which may suggest that the term "Islamophobia" should be dropped in favour of "anti-Muslim hatred".

I began this chapter with that alarming quotation from Blaise Pascal. How astonishing that such a committed Christian could say such a thing. But it is a reminder that any good thing is capable of corruption and distortion. An example might be found in the Crusades which some think can be justified in terms of access to the holy sites of Jerusalem and freedom of faith. But nothing can justify the murders, the killings, the rapes, the theft and terror that those calling themselves Christians committed in the name of Christ. It is a period in Western history of which we should be deeply ashamed. In the same way, Islamist terrorists, most of them motivated by their faith, have destroyed countless lives through deadly attacks on innocent civilians.

I am convinced that three features of dialogue should guide us all as Islam roots itself into Western societies. First, Muslim members of secular societies have a duty to obey the laws wherever they settle. While this is an obvious observation it must be emphasised again and again. There can be no preferential treatment for Islam in Western societies. Somehow a balance has to be found between the assimilation model that is seen in France and the multiculturalism that is typical of Britain and the United States. In France, the insistence that every migrant must eventually accept the secular norms of the nation has led to widespread disobedience by Muslim believers with dangerous levels of hostility towards Western ideals. The fact that in 2020 about 76 mosques were investigated for showing radical tendencies is indicative of French concern that Muslim communities do not drift away from the nation's "laïque" model.

In the UK the model of multiculturalism – live and let live – has not stopped radicalism developing. It is clear that radicalism feeds off tolerance and grows where laws are weak. And yet the claim that multiculturalism encourages cultural segregation leading to violence is not as applicable as it might seem when we ask: "What about closed Jewish communities in parts of north London, Hindu families in Leicester or rich, gated white communities around Guildford?" Do we suspect them too of harbouring terrorists and encouraging radical thought?

Clearly the issues are more subtle than simply pointing to cultural models as the sole reasons for radicalisation. Indeed, we often find poverty, poor education, unemployment and isolation (often of the female members of families) in these radicalised communities. These key elements should be given more attention.

Second, there must be no wavering about the subservience of sharia law to civic law. Earlier in this chapter I spoke of the alarm that was created in the UK when Rowan Williams raised, tentatively, the question concerning embracing sharia law within civic law. The reason why I and many others resisted this suggestion related to different perspectives between Christianity and Islam concerning the nature of religious law. It was Christ himself who separated faith from human law in his oft-quoted "render unto Caesar that which is Caesar's and unto God that which is God's" (Mark 12:17). This phrase has become a summary of the relationship between human law and Christian discipleship. Islam allows no such distinction and separation because Islam is a self-contained and fully articulated vision for the complete ordering of society and of every human life. It is important, therefore, to recognise the missionary impulse of Islam in the fusing of politics and faith. I recall the friendly yet tense discussions I had with Sheikh Mohammed Sayyid Tantawi, Rector of Al-Azhar University in Cairo. Although he was regarded by some as a moderate voice within Sunni Islam, his vision was the eventual conversion of the world to Islam. Whilst I could not object to such a desire, because I, as a Christian, long that all should embrace the truths of Christianity, our fundamental difference lay in the nature of our founders. The Islamic prophet Muhammad's desire was for the submission of all to Allah. Jesus, however, looked into the eyes of Pilate and said, "My kingdom is not of this world." (John 18:36) Muhammad never made such a statement; Islam's desire is to conquer the world.

Returning then to the place of sharia in Western society, whilst, clearly, every religion has the right to expect its followers to adhere to its faith, no religion has the right to demand equality for itself and then impose restrictions on its own members against their will in an open society. Sharia laws that penalise women, for example, are clearly wrong in terms of natural justice. It is discriminatory that in matters of inheritance a woman's portion is only half that of a man's and that the testimony of women in legal matters has only half the weight of men's. We must all challenge such denigration of half of the human family.

Third, Western civilisation must bring to the dialogue with a resurgent Islam not a vague tolerance of all things so that, in effect, anything goes, but clear convictions of equality, freedom and toleration. Almost a century ago T.E. Hulme wrote:

> In the history of every civilisation a time comes when
> the race loses confidence in its gods, its values and its

mission; and then, in some way not understood, it begins to die out and less civilised races take its place. In Western Europe today there is a decline in courage, faith and hope that seems exactly like the decline that led to the fall of Athens, Sparta and Rome.[11]

The historian R.G. Collingwood wrote similarly:

Civilisations sometimes perish because they are forcibly broken up by the armed attack of enemies without or revolutionaries within, but never from this cause alone. Such attacks never succeed unless the thing that is attacked is weakened by doubt as to whether the end which it sets before itself, the form of life which it tries to realise, is worth achieving. On the other hand, this doubt is quite capable of destroying a civilisation without any help whatever. If the people who share a civilisation are no longer on the whole convinced that the form of life which it tries to realise is worth realising, nothing can save it.[12]

5

Among the Very Poor

The aim of the Bank is to put a smile on the face of a child.

Jim Wolfensohn

It has been my privilege, shared with Eileen, to have worked among the very poor of the world. Coming from a rich country like Britain nothing can really prepare one for abject poverty. Of course, poverty exists in the United Kingdom and in all advanced countries, but it is foolish to lump the two kinds of poverty together. Abject poverty is to live on under one dollar a day with no other support structures; rags for clothes; tarpaulin, if you are lucky, for a roof; little access to education and certainly no benefit system. If you are a woman or a girl, your future is even more wretched. I grew up in a poor English family but never experienced the devastation of absolute poverty.

I began to take a close interest in the global problem of poverty as my visits to different parts of the Anglican Communion progressed. The role of Archbishop of Canterbury makes it impossible for the occupant to be an expert in any dimension of social concern. But what one acquires is a sense of the scale of social issues and the impact of the decisions made by richer nations on very poor nations. As I visited Papua New Guinea, South Sudan, Madagascar, Kenya, Uganda, South Africa and many other African countries I returned home with distressing memories of suffering people: that tall Dinka girl, about my older daughter's age, with two babies at her breast who called across from behind two brutal Sudanese guards, "Archbishop, please help us! We have no food, we have nothing; I want to go home!" I felt helpless, I could do nothing for her. I will never forget her. Similarly, I can never forget sitting in the back of the car of the High Commissioner going from the airport to the Residence. While we were stopped at the lights, a young woman appeared at my car window. A small boy was on her hips. She was emaciated and very frail. I was about to let down the window when the High Commissioner said sharply: "No, Archbishop. It is our policy never to respond to beggars." As I had no money on me, there was no point in doing anything other than look abject poverty in the eye – and turn away my gaze.

But it was a telephone call in late 1997 that led to a major shift in my approach to the poor: from the wringing of hands to real engagement. A senior World Bank official contacted my office to put me in touch with the new President of the World Bank, Jim Wolfensohn.[13] Indeed, I knew of him and all I had read impressed me. A few years my senior in age, he was Jewish by faith and an Australian by birth. He had had a successful career as a lawyer and investment banker and had even established his own investment firm. He had also been an Olympic fencer. Thus the picture I had formed of him was of an outstanding human being born with a silver spoon in his mouth. That was not so. He grew up in a modest family with few privileges. His parents had emigrated from London to Australia shortly before Jim's birth. He was brought up in a two-bedroom flat in Edgecliff, a district of Sydney. His father, a failed businessman, struggled to find employment. Jim would say later in his autobiography that monetary insecurity became the driving force of his life. The successes he had obtained he had achieved by hard work. Jim Wolfensohn, nominated by President Clinton to the Presidency of the World Bank, was determined to think outside the box and make a success of his new job.

What essentially is the World Bank? It is not a bank as we understand it, but rather a dedicated global partnership to fight poverty throughout the world. With 189 member countries and offices in over 130 locations the World Bank is a powerful instrument for changing lives. In Jim's eyes, all was not well with an organisation under political attack. From the left, anti-globalisation groups slammed the Bank as nothing more than an extension of US foreign policy. From the right, it was criticised as an inefficient source of handouts to poorly performing countries.

During Jim Wolfensohn's two terms as president the culture of the World Bank was profoundly changed. He made the Bank independent of political interference and he shattered the taboo held within some sections of the Bank that corruption was a price that had to be paid to get aid to the very poor. In a speech in 1999 he said: "When I arrived at the Bank I was told 'you don't talk about the C-word because it is a political issue. The Bank is owned by governments, and the charter does not allow you to enter the political field.'" Jim, not afraid of controversy, addressed this problem early on in his role as president. He argued that corruption is not a neutral act that oils the machine, but a practice that literally takes money and resources away from the people the Bank was set up to help. From now on, the President declared, any sign of corruption would rule out any organisation or business from working with the bank.

Jim was also the first President to engage deliberately with faith leaders – a deed that would put him at odds with the Board of the World Bank. At our first meeting, he told me that on becoming President of the World Bank he discovered from his first visit to Tanzania that nearly half of all health care, education and social care in the country was delivered through the churches and other faith groups. Jim said he found himself asking: "Why are we processing all World Bank grants through the government and ignoring the extensive religious networks of the country?"

It was this capacity to question current ways of doing things that alarmed his senior colleagues at the World Bank. What worried them specially was his willingness to form links and relationships with religious leaders. But why did he choose to begin with the Archbishop of Canterbury and the Anglican Communion, instead of the more powerful Catholic Church with the most senior religious figure of all, the Pope? I never did get a clear answer to that question. It is most likely the case that he chose a more flexible vehicle for what he wanted to do, as well as the strong personal relationship that he and I were able to forge together. For he and I got on well even though Jim had a very short fuse and, typically of an Australian, was blunt and to the point. Anger in a leader is not an entirely negative emotion. Jesus expressed anger at times in the face of hypocrisy and wrong. We should get angry and depressed when confronted by the poor being victimised or the hungry unfed. But uncontrolled anger often undermines unity and teamwork and destroys relationships. Much as I appreciated Jim's determination to get things done, I was concerned by the way he rode roughshod over well-meaning people who happened to be junior employees. Although this disturbed me I had no right to interfere in staff relationships. Indeed I was thrilled to meet a leader who really wanted to make a difference, and his bluntness helped to cut to the heart of issues.

In February 1998 an extraordinary gathering of religious leaders met the President of the World Bank at Lambeth Palace. Nine world religions were represented: Baha'is, Buddhists, Christians, Hindus, Jains, Jews, Muslims, Sikhs and Taoists. All manner of dress expressed the richness of diversity, and the seniority of all participants indicated the importance each faith community considered the conference to have. Pope John Paul II was represented by Cardinal Etchegaray, the retired Archbishop of Marseille, a distinguished and wise man whose presence graced the conference. Chief Rabbi Jonathan Sacks was also present with other senior rabbis.

Jim and I had decided that we would chair this jointly and we encouraged the delegates to speak frankly. And they did. What came across powerfully was the anger of some religious communities towards the World Bank. Some, especially those from Asia, saw the bank as a great secular evil inflicted on the very poor which, with its programme of structural adjustment programmes (SAP) and rigid policies, did more harm than good. But, as well as anger, there were moments of humour also. One African church leader from the Côte d'Ivoire very wittily compared the World Bank to a pangolin, a creature resembling a cross between an ant-eater and an armadillo that lives in deep holes in forests and is rarely seen. The speaker continued: "The visit of a World Bank official to our country is rather like the appearance of the pangolin. When he appears everyone gathers around to admire the strange creature." This politely expressed the sentiment "Where have you been all the time?" and was a friendly way of reminding the World Bank that intermittent visits could never replace those present all the time with poor communities.

The President listened attentively to the criticism, but I could tell that he was exercising a great deal of self-control in mastering his temper. A forthright Indian lady had just commented that the World Bank was the "mother and godmother of all banks" when Jim interrupted the tirade with an explosion of his own:

> But we are not a bank! We are the largest foreign aid agency in the world and owned by all the governments, including your own. The World Bank has no money of its own and what it has comes from your governments and we are accountable to your governments. If you think that the bank tries to feather its own nest by extracting money from the world's poor, you have completely the wrong idea. The bank exists for one purpose only – it wants to bring people out of poverty. Of course we make mistakes, and part of the reason why we are having this conference is to find ways of learning from one another.

That tough exchange did not signal the closure of the conference – which it so easily could have done – but rather was the beginning of frank appraisals of the strengths and weaknesses of both religious communities and the bank and International Monetary Fund (IMF). There was recognition that the bank and other secular agencies had been guilty in the past of neglecting the role of faith in conflict resolution, poverty reduction and advocacy. Jim and others were clear that religious communities were already contributing a great deal towards development and were the closest to the very poor. They were active in health care and provision of education and in building community. They gave poor people dignity and hope – in short, the World Bank had woken up to the great potential in faith communities.

However, it was noted that religious communities were not without their deficiencies. One of Jim's senior assistants pointed out a structural problem with faith communities. They were admittedly very close to the most vulnerable, especially women and children, but traditional attitudes to the role of women often prohibited the necessary changes that were urgently required to empower women – in education, contraception and work. An equally serious criticism was that the bank's experience of faith groups had shown that some were seen as "survival oriented" rather than "transformative institutions" and, when that happened, some churches turned inward to care only for their members and not for the community.

Another person observed that the World Bank's non-confessional and secular agenda limited its concepts of human needs to poverty and, instead of affirming the importance of community that is so essential to the African and Eastern understanding of life, seemed in danger of undermining it through its focus on the individual. The bank's understanding of "prosperity", one religious leader argued, seemed solely "money oriented".

What was remarkable in the cool, rational and clinical critique of both the bank and religious communities was the way it cleared the air and enabled both sides to go deeper into issues of development. Neither side had all the resources and answers. If we cared for others, we had to work together.

The religious leaders recognised the extraordinary nature of the meeting: that the President of the World Bank had chosen to invite them and was there arguing with them. The mood of the meeting changed from anger to deep appreciation of Jim Wolfensohn's personal commitment to work with faith communities.

From that historic encounter the World Faiths Development Dialogue emerged, with the President and myself as co-founders. Our communiqué declared:

> This has been a precious opportunity for frank and intensive dialogue between religious leaders and development experts, drawn from nine of the world's religious faiths and leading staff of the World Bank... we are strengthened in our conviction that the definition and practice of desirable development must have regard to spiritual, ethical, environmental, cultural and social considerations, if it is to be sustainable and contribute to the well-being of all, especially the poorest and weakest members of society.

It was agreed that WFDD would not be an "aid-granting" body but one that sought to maximise the considerable but unrealised potential of faith communities around the world. Its task should be to bring faith groups together to do more in eradicating poverty, and through development to deepen existing dialogue and thus overcoming conflict and misunderstanding. A very light and flexible steering group was formed and it was charged to work with poor communities in empowering them to work more closely with World Bank officials and NGO groups.

Jim and I were delighted with the success of the meeting and, within a few months, were able to see significant progress made. We received considerable financial support from the Aga Khan and much encouragement from the Duke of Edinburgh Prince Philip and Prince Hassan of Jordan. The incomparable Dr Haruhisa Handa, a Shinto priest and businessman (a seemingly unlikely combination), gave generous support as well. And then the bombshell. The World Bank Board refused to endorse this unique agreement between the World Bank and religious communities.

The French representative particularly objected to such a liaison, arguing that the principle of separation of Church and State forbade such collaboration. That argument won the day and the President was instructed to break off all official links with the World Faiths Development Dialogue. Jim was deeply upset and outraged but there was little he could do. He made it clear, however, that he would personally continue as an individual as co-Chair but he could not continue in his official capacity. While I was delighted that Jim in his own right would continue, the blockage imposed by the Board meant that we could not depend upon the resources of the World Bank in the continuation of the work. Like Jim, I grieved over this appalling short-sightedness. The irony was that on September 12th 2001, the day after 9/11, several members of the same Board said to Jim that the previous day's events had shown the importance of the initiative. "We must draw religious communities into closer collaboration with the Bank," a number of bank officials declared.

Sadly, the initiative which offered so much promise never really got off the ground in the way that Jim and I had intended, hindered as it was by the intransigence of the Board of the World Bank. This was a striking example of the woeful ignorance of secular leadership, particularly Western leadership, in its failure to see the power of faith groups through their closeness to the very poor. It was a reality that the majority of the Board of the World Bank failed to see. As a senior Ugandan stated, "Religion is inextricably woven into every aspect of life in Uganda. For most Ugandans, religious beliefs play a major role in their sense of personal identity, their thought patterns, and their moral judgments." That could well sum up Africa as a whole. Jim was able to see that better than most. Although he was not a practising Jew, he was respectful of faith and an admirer of the power of religious communities to deliver aid. For him, as for me, faith communities were under-valued partners in the fight against injustice, poverty, war and disease. The plain truth is that the religious illiteracy of most political leaders, especially in the West, holds back development and weakens aid getting to the people who need it most.

However, even though WFDD was cut off at its knees by the failure of the Bank to see the potential of a partnership with religious communities, three very significant Leaders' Meetings were to yield great fruit. The first took place in 2002 at Canterbury Cathedral in my final year as Archbishop. One of the most pressing issues of the 90s was the cancellation of debt, an issue of major importance for the poorest countries with implications for the richest. We gathered to address this issue. It was a glittering gathering of the powerful that met in the new International Centre adjacent to the majestic cathedral, the home of Anglicanism worldwide. The power of Jim's name as President of the World Bank was sufficient to draw together outstanding people from the world of politics, religion, banking, charities and entertainment. Famous as the lead singer of U2, Bono's commitment to the poor was known, and his passionate speech calling for a change of heart was a call that inspired us all. Indeed, on every occasion I heard Bono speak I was moved and amazed by his articulacy and power. The gift of music given abundantly to him was matched by his passion for the poor. He could have graced any pulpit in the world.

Clare Short, Minister for Development in Tony Blair's government, was also a force to be reckoned with. I had previously worked with Lynda Chalker MP who had served with distinction in the same office in John Major's team. Both women were impressive people who, though they might differ in temperament and political idealism, were equally committed to making a difference to the world. Clare Short was Secretary of State for Development from 1997 to 2003. I had great admiration for her. We did not always agree; indeed, she had strong views and expressed them firmly but malice was never intended. She cared deeply about her work and endeavoured to make a real difference. Although she described herself as a lapsed Catholic, the foundations of her compassion were profoundly Christian. From her many travels to poor countries she saw the significance of faith communities and what they could do. Clare also saw clearly the significance of WFDD and was a great support. She was, however, very critical of what she viewed as an emotional response to debt forgiveness from church groups. Her candid remarks on the popular Jubilee 2000 movement was that it was far too "pious": where there is debt, someone has to pay for it for debt does not mysteriously vanish. I happened to share that view myself, although I also took the view that the richer nations could do and should do more in terms of debt relief and the deferment of owed money. More than a few poor nations owed so much that new borrowings were eaten up by the need to make payments on the loans they had already taken out. It was a frightening vicious circle that imprisoned the very poor. In her presentation at the Canterbury meeting Clare agreed that something had to be done. It was immoral, for example, that present day South Africa, transformed by Nelson Mandela's policies, should have to pay back borrowed money that had been used to repress the people long ago. Clare Short left no one in doubt that although she had great sympathy with debt cancellation, with some reservations, it was not the total answer to the grave problem of the crushing burden of debt. It had to be considered not on its own but in the context of reform, growth and investment.

The Canterbury discussion was an important moment of clarity on the issue of debt relief and cancellation. The senior religious leaders present were informed about the economic factors that politicians had to confront. The more worldly-wise politicians and economists present were made aware of the distress of the very poor through the advocacy of faith leaders. Jim Wolfensohn, as President of the World Bank, would later say to me that the Canterbury Leaders' Conference was a step towards the initiative developed by the World Bank and the IMF known as the Heavily Indebted Poor Countries initiative (HIPC). Clare Short would later become a key player in getting the HIPC initiative supported. She persuaded Oxfam International to do a lot of the basic arithmetic on debt relief, which she used to convince donors of their duty to agree.

Thirty-seven nations were selected as a pilot group, all characterised by low GDP and a heavy debt burden combined with unsustainable levels of poverty. The development of this policy revealed the simplism of calling for 100 per cent debt cancellation alone. As the President of the World Bank himself argued, how can you expect lenders of credit to borrowers to accept that they might not get full repayment of their loan? No government, no business will tolerate that.[14]

But the logic of compassion clearly necessitated some debt cancellation, albeit set within a comprehensive strategy rooted in open markets, responsible governments and more decisive support from the international community.

It has worked. Since the establishing of the HIPC scheme huge steps in economic reform have taken place. More people are out of dire poverty now than there have ever been. Although this has been a painful and often slow development, the world community can take some pleasure in the spectacular progress made.

The Canterbury Leaders' meeting also addressed the crisis created by the HIV/AIDS epidemic. We had good cause to do so because faith communities, representing as they do the interests of the very poor, were caught up by the impact of this cruel disease. We had with us Canon Gideon Byamugisha. Gideon, a tall, distinguished and well-educated Ugandan, had been ordained in 1992, following the death of his wife in 1991. On being told that his wife had been tested positive for HIV shortly before dying, he went to be tested and found out that he too was HIV positive. For three years Gideon lived with the news, wondering about the implications of telling others. Eventually he went to see his bishop who encouraged him to be an advocate for AIDS sufferers. This he did, becoming the first practising priest in Africa to break the silence and to confront the stigma of the disease. Gideon's contribution enabled us to focus on what the faith communities may do together to face the shame caused by the disease. Indeed, Uganda, as a country, was among the first of the nations to reach beyond the issue of stigma and concentrate upon helping the victims to regain their dignity and self-worth. Gideon was not the only champion. Another courageous Ugandan leader was Philly Lutaaya, a very popular musician who used his fame to confront the fear of HIV. Lutaaya died before antiviral drugs were available but his celebration of life raised, with Gideon's influence, the attitude of the people. Uganda became one of the earliest countries to emerge positively from the disease. The conference was able to recognise strong influence of Gideon whom the UN would later call "a truly brave son of Africa".

The Canterbury Leaders' Conference was a triumph and the work of WFDD continued to flourish. Jim began to take more of a back seat on our fledgling organisation and Ms Katherine Marshall, one of Jim's senior advisers, was seconded to be the new CEO of the World Faiths Development Dialogue. Katherine was and is an outstanding thinker and leader in the world of aid. She was widely respected, having devoted most of her career to the World Bank.

A second initiative in London was to make a surprising impact. In 2004, with the enthusiastic agreement of Gordon Brown, Chancellor of the Exchequer, an international gathering of development experts, senior politicians, academics and journalists assembled at the Treasury to discuss world poverty. The one-day event was organised by Lord Griffiths of Fforestfach and myself. Brian Griffiths had been a significant member of Margaret Thatcher's inner circle of advisers as Chair of her Policy Unit. Brian was also chairman of a small organisation of senior Christian men and women known as Christian Responsibility in Public Affairs (CRPA). The group existed to give spiritual support to all Christians in public office. I became an unofficial chaplain to this largely lay group. Brian and I quickly became firm friends. We approached the Chancellor to see if he was willing to use his authority and offices for a gathering of economists, politicians and faith leaders to assess progress made in poverty reduction.

Gordon Brown not only leapt at this opportunity to show his support but also largely underwrote the costs. Throughout his time in office he consistently endeavoured to bring people together, and deserves praise for his awareness of the power of churches and faith communities. During his years in office he had regular breakfast meetings with leaders of mainstream churches. But the gathering in May 2004 was of a different and significant order – it was international, it was public and it was held at the Treasury, the symbol of mammon. Present and taking part were leaders of the calibre of President Lulu of Brazil, Bono, Jim Wolfensohn, Hilary Benn and many faith leaders. This gathering at the Treasury signalled that engagement with issues of poverty was a moral necessity.

A two-fold challenge emerged from that brief conference. The first was addressed to the rich nations of the world. Gordon Brown issued a warning that "without a substantial transfer of additional resources from the richest to the poorest countries in the form of investment for development the long term causes of poverty cannot be solved". The second was a challenge to religions themselves that they also had to change attitudes if they wanted their rhetoric about assisting the poor to match reality. A fundamental element was the position and role of women. How may societies that have traditionally discriminated against women – sometimes in the name of religion – achieve a higher degree of equality? It is heartening to know that major faiths are beginning to change their behaviour in order to adapt to new situations and opportunities, but there is still a very long way to go. Such gatherings of politicians, faith leaders and others, like those that met at the Treasury, are significant moments that move the debate along but they are only steps along the way. Hearts have to be moved before wills are engaged and it continues to be a long process. But it is happening and the gap between the very poor and the wealthy is narrowing.

The gathering at the Treasury was, in fact, an important step towards the next Leaders' Meeting which took place at the end of January 2005 at Dublin Castle. It was an ironically significant place for such a meeting. Dublin Castle had fulfilled a number of roles through its long history from its Irish roots, the English conquest, British rule and then from 1922 the seat of the Irish Free State. We were welcomed very charmingly by the President of Ireland, Mary McAleese. Then, together with Roman Catholic Archbishop of Dublin and Primate of Ireland, Diarmuid Martin, the President of the World Bank and I shared the leadership of the conference. Diarmuid, an old friend, was a very well-known and respected leader in the world of development.

It is a fact that, when international gatherings of this kind meet, urgent topical matters rise to the surface and have a habit of dominating. This happened at Dublin Castle. The international body representing different fields of interest found itself confronting not only the urgent matter of HIV/AIDS but also the aftermath of the tsunami which had hit India, Sri Lanka, Indonesia and other nations only five weeks earlier – along with issues of poverty, education and women's issues. The demand to make HIV the sole issue for our gathering had to be resisted and to be put into the context of care for all. Jim Wolfensohn in his presidential address focused on the issue of "equity" – that we lived in a world dangerously out of balance. The numbers, he said, are brutal and frightening. Some 1.2 billion people live on less than one dollar a day and close to three billion live on less than two dollars a day. More than 115 million children do not have the chance to go to school. Over 40 million people are HIV positive and over three million died of HIV/Aids in 2004. Jim's speech was passionate and convincing.

In my speech I raised the moral issues that such figures spell. The issue facing us, I said, is not only the misery that lies behind the figures but also the moral imperative to address the matter of fairness in terms of access to a decent life and access to education as well as the challenge of poverty. I drew upon the implications of the tsunami which was shockingly indiscriminate in its devastation. About half the victims were children. Towns were not destroyed; they simply vanished. The tsunami mocked the puny efforts of human beings as well as our hubris in assuming that we are all-powerful. Nevertheless, brought down to earth by the power and randomness of nature, the goodwill and generosity of the world was swift in its compassion and response. The rebuilding had started immediately and religious communities, strongly represented among the poor, were central to renewal.

HIV/AIDS was, however, a different reality. The Canterbury Leaders' Conference had addressed the disease because it was still a major concern that was destroying so many lives. We had to recognise that in the early days of the pandemic some Christian leaders and politicians had turned their back on sufferings arising from what they saw as moral shortcomings. HIV issued, as they saw it, from sinful behaviour and promiscuity. Thus, initially the Church gave uncertain leadership instead of the compassion and care that was desperately required. Sadly, Canon Gideon Byamugisha was not able to be with us although his influence was tangible. However, we were not lacking experts.

A number of clear factors emerged from our discussion: the feminisation of HIV/AIDS, the predominant role of faith institutions in orphan care, the issue of sexual abstinence as well as the geographic patterns of the disease. Bono sent a powerful message, as did Mario Giro, a leader of the Community of Sant' Egidio, Rome. A major consideration was the fact that gender inequality had helped to spread HIV around the world. From Ted Karpf of the World Health Organisation came the observation that women are biologically, epidemiologically and socio-economically more vulnerable to the ravages of HIV/AIDS. They were shockingly disadvantaged and unsupported. Admonitions to young women in developing countries to marry resulted in a cruel irony: they often became more at risk when they did so. A single girl may have greater power to assert herself and resist sexual advances; but as a married woman, she was at the mercy of her husband who was more likely to engage in extra-marital activity.

The Dublin Leaders' Conference was a significant step towards a closer partnership between religious communities, charites and aid agencies, diplomats and politicians. In 2005 antiretroviral drugs were just beginning to emerge and today, some fifteen years on, the situation is radically changed. Drugs to suppress HIV infections are now widely available. Known as HAART (Highly Active Antiretroviral Therapy), this "cocktail" has enabled millions of people to live with AIDS. Canon Gideon Byamugisha, in Uganda, is still leading a fulfilled life, working with those suffering from AIDS and giving them a sense of purpose.

The Dublin Conference was Jim's last public appearance as

co-Chair of WFDD as he was stepping down from the World Bank as President.

Throughout the period of my office as Archbishop and since, the issue of climate change and the serious environmental damage caused has been a growing concern. In 1992 the UN Rio Summit met and expressed profound concern about the "dangerous" human interference in the climate system, recognising that climate change was now a matter of global concern. Other major meetings took place in 1995, 1997 (the first legally binding climate treaty), 2001, 2005 and 2007, leading up to the Paris Agreement of 2019.

Al Gore, former Vice President of the United States, made a major contribution in 2006 when he said at the screening of *An Inconvenient Truth* that "each passing day brings yet more evidence that we are facing a planetary emergency – a crisis that threatens the survival of our civilisation and the habitability of the earth". What has been truly depressing is the indifference of many in the West to the incontrovertible evidence of global warming and the dire consequences for us all, particularly the very poor.

During the last two decades there has been one religious leader who has consistently drawn attention to the ecological damage that human beings are doing to our fragile planet. That voice has been the leader of the Eastern Orthodox Churches, His All-Holiness Ecumenical Patriarch Bartholomew. His concerns have included the link between climate change and sustainable development. Naturally he is not the only church leader to express considerable concern at the damage human beings are causing the environment, but his voice has been consistent and compelling. He has welcomed the way that millions of people have been brought out of poverty but observes that, unless our behaviour is changed, with the incalculable harm we – and particularly the West – are doing to creation, millions are likely to be dragged back into grinding poverty again.

In 2009 I was able to see something of the degradation of nature and the way that climate change was hampering poverty reduction when, as Vice President of Tearfund, I visited Yei in South Sudan. This was my fifth visit to Sudan, a land that Eileen and I came to love

– especially its joyful and resilient people. Yei, sharing its southern border with Uganda and the Democratic Republic of Congo, is a bustling town 110 miles south of Juba. The main reason for our visit was to see some exciting work of Tearfund in development and also to meet the bishops of Sudan and share with them.

Flying in on the tiny MAF plane from Juba to Yei enabled us to see the beauty of the land beneath with the scattered groups of huts denoting human habitation. But what was immediately obvious was the dryness of the landscape, the dried up rivers and streams and the scorched earth. On landing we were taken to a new church community centre where, for once, the toilets actually worked. However, ominously, we saw a familiar sight in noticing some twenty men sitting around a well with scores of screws, tools and parts of the mechanism scattered around. We were there for four days and never did get a hot shower. This was yet another image of Africa – willing people but basic technology had not reached them.

The first part of my programme was a real joy as we met outstanding bishops such as Archbishop Daniel Deng, Archbishop of Sudan, and Hilary, the Bishop of Yei, as well as some twenty or so other bishops. All were accompanied by their wives who were delighted to see Eileen and to share with her.

We then visited some of the surrounding villages to see Tearfund's innovative work. This included an impressive visit to Goja where a partnership with DfID (the UK government's Department for International Development) was helping to build a well and a mobile clinic. However, what important organisations such as DfID and the World Bank cannot do is to supply the manpower that actually changes the lives of people. This, in Africa, is the real strength of the Church on the ground. I have already referred to the sad image of the men sitting around a new well unable to repair it – but the shortage of basic technology is beginning to be addressed. I saw the evidence in the work of Tearfund and its sister charity ACROSS. The educative programme is called PAP – Participatory Awakening Process. Apart from the irritating jargon of all these initials, so common in the world of development, the energy and ability shown by the young leaders from as far afield as Uganda, Kenya, and Britain, was an inspiring example of Christian compassion in action. The genius of PAP was its rejection of a top-down approach to aid. The very people being helped were engaged in the process of decision-making and change. The result was there in the formation of farmers' groups, loan sharing and the creation of cooperatives. Instead of working alone on a subsistence basis many farmers now found their income increasing by sharing resources. In Goja village the Manga group – fifteen women and seventeen men – sold ninety-one bags of maize, generating an income of 4,550 Sudanese pounds.

But I was left in no doubt about the impact of climate change on southern Sudan. At Juba airport I saw a sign stating that climate change is the "No 1 danger in South Sudan". Since the mid-70s South Sudan has experienced an average decline of around 15 per cent precipitation, as well as increased variability in the amount and timing of rainfall. Along with the decline in rainfall, related issues such as pests and disease add to the environmental problems.

Our journey then took us to west Kenya where further examples of PAP were seen. In villages such as Wanguru, Chuka, Ntimene, Meru and Rung 'Ang we saw other examples of cooperatives in action. Many of them were led and organised by powerful and effective women of all ages. In several of these places PAP had morphed into PRA (Participatory Rural Appraisal) to build strong communities to combat disease and climate change. In many of these villages the focus was upon health care, especially childbirth. Women who, tragically, often have such a raw deal in poor communities, were taking the lead. The Anglican Church of Kenya was doing a splendid job developing the role and position of women. I was so glad that Eileen and I were able to call in on David Gitari, former Archbishop of Kenya, now quite old and frail, but his sharp intelligence and great sense of humour were still on display. The visit to Yei and west Kenya, and further forays to central Africa and Rwanda, brought home to me that the future of Africa lay in the hands of women. Men have largely failed them; they must take responsibility for their destinies and their families. I am certain they can do it.

My work among the very poor still continues at the age of 85 but now at a more distant level. I am physically unable to function at the same level any longer but I still chair the World Faiths Development Dialogue, and our work is an important strand in the worldwide fight to give all children a dignified start to life. When Christian communities fail to do this they forfeit their right to be called followers of Jesus Christ. Jim Wolfensohn, who died in November 2020 and whom I last saw in a wheelchair earlier that year, had one simple but great ambition – it was to put a smile on the face of all poor children. I share that dream too.

6

The Fires of Conflict

*What difference does it make to the dead, the orphans
and the homeless, whether the mad destruction is
wrought under the name of totalitarianism, or in the
holy name of liberty or democracy?*

Mahatma Gandhi

Conflicts in any area of life may take several forms. They can be
calm as well as contentious, benign as well as bitter. However,
whatever form they take, leadership is challenged and the character of the organisation is revealed. Three important conflicts came
in retirement in which I was deeply and emotionally involved.

The first was beginning to disturb me when I retired in
November 2002. I was troubled because I was aware that one
important unresolved issue threatened to challenge and divide
the Anglican Communion. It was the matter of the ordination of
homosexual people. The Lambeth Conference of 1998 over which
I had presided had been hugely successful in many respects, but
Resolution Lambeth 1.10 which declared homosexual acts "sinful"
was a time bomb waiting to explode. Even though the resolution
was overwhelmingly carried, and backed by a commitment to keep

listening to one another, only an extremely naïve person at the time would have felt that was sufficient. The American bishops, angry and hurt, returned home determined to pursue their own pathway. It was hardly a surprise, therefore, when within a few months Gene Robinson, a highly popular and charismatic gay clergyman, was chosen by the diocese of New Hampshire to be its bishop. Huge dismay greeted this decision, not only in the wider Communion but also in America.

Robinson was duly installed on November 3rd 2003. The excitement was huge, with three hundred press people present along with forty-eight bishops and a congregation of three thousand. Robinson wore a bulletproof vest and security was tight. There was little that my successor, Rowan Williams, could do to slow down the process, and in any case he, temperamentally and theologically, possibly had more sympathy than I with the decision. But everyone knew that this was a major step towards the breakup of the Anglican Communion. Both Rowan and I had deep conversations with Frank Griswold, the Presiding Bishop of the Episcopal Church in the USA, about the decision. Frank, a very good friend, and a holy and wise man, was quite clear and firm that this was the right decision for his House of Bishops and General Convention. Recognising how this would damage the wider Church and harm the fragile bonds of unity – let alone the humanitarian damage done to the most vulnerable and poor people in the developing world by the split – everyone was deeply concerned about the consequences.

I had to consider carefully my own responsibilities towards The Episcopal Church (TEC) and the unity of the Anglican Communion. My opposition to the ordination of practising homosexuals was well known, but I was reluctant to be seen to be a campaigner on this issue. Retirement for me meant retirement. I felt it would be irresponsible to carry on a private campaign after leaving office. In many ways I respected homosexuals who desired to serve Christ in his church; indeed, when we put Lambeth 1.10 to the Lambeth Conference it was on the basis that the debate was not over; we needed to do more work and live together in understanding and affection. But Robinson's ordination changed everything, leading to churches breaking away from TEC and new denominations being created. The tug to join in this and support the breakaway churches was seductive but it had to be resisted. I made it clear to Frank Griswold that, as a former archbishop, I would continue to support TEC's wider mission within the Communion whenever possible, and particularly those churches within it that took a traditional point of view and which did not want to be forced to leave.

Our visits to America and elsewhere in the Communion continued and we were glad to make ourselves available. In later 2004 I was invited by a young minister in Pensacola, Florida, to visit his parish for a few days. I contacted a close friend, Dr Paul Zahl, to get his view on this visit and he was enthusiastic: "The Rev Dr Russ Levenson," Paul stated, "is an outstanding priest who would value a visit. He is quite capable of becoming one of the most effective leaders of the American Church." We were impressed by Paul's support for a young man in his forties and accepted the invitation which took place in February 2005.

And what a visit it turned out to be. As I frequently found when invited to the States, the itinerary was not easy. We started in Fairhope where I preached several times for Mark Wilson, a dear friend, at Christ Church; then to Birmingham, Alabama where I preached at the cathedral and had talks with the bishop; then on to Pensacola to spend several days with Russ Levenson and Laura, his wife. Hurricane Ivan had hit Pensacola three months earlier and the devastation was appalling. Some 25,000 homes had been destroyed and the bell tower of Christ Church, Russ's church, had collapsed into the main building, wiping out one third of the nave. A temporary wall had to be built, but within two weeks worship had resumed. The bishop's house was spectacularly hit, so much so that the bishop was living in temporary accommodation.

To say I was impressed by Russ's approach and ministry is an understatement. His workload was intense and he expected his visiting preachers to go flat out as well. The schedule was unrelenting, yet enjoyable – it was easy to understand why Russ's ministry was popular. Although Russ was as orthodox as I on the issue of the ordination of practising gay people he was determined not to be distracted from his principal commitment to get on with the job of ministry and serving faithfully.

In May 2007, we were back in Pensacola at Russ's invitation to confirm some forty-eight people and to speak at a Patrons' dinner. This coincided with an invitation to preach at the famous naval airbase and the annual Golden Eagles Service where we met astronauts Neil Armstrong and Jim Lovell and their wives. Golden Eagles was the generic name given to outstanding naval pilots, from which body many astronauts were chosen. We had drinks with both men and discussed their careers. Of the two, Jim was the more forthcoming about the nature of his faith and what it meant to him. Neil seemed shyer but equally friendly.

The friendship with Russ and Laura deepened as the degree of our common love for faith and unity deepened. He was clearly being seen as a leader for a much larger church than that in Pensacola. I was therefore not surprised when I was approached by the wardens of St Martin's Houston to give a reference for Russ whom they were considering as the next rector of this large and influential church. He was inevitably offered the post and I was invited to preach at his installation on January 6th 2008.

What I was unprepared for was that St Martin's Church was also the place of worship for George Bush, Sr, 41st President of the USA and his wife, Barbara. Not only so, but Jim Baker III, a former White House Chief of Staff and Secretary of State, and his wife Susan were also regular worshippers at St Martin's. By this time Russ had already struck up a firm friendship with the Bush family and we met them for dinner on January 4th at the Country Club. The President entered on sticks having had a fall a few days earlier but otherwise was in very good form. Both George Bush, Sr, and Barbara were charming and approachable people. This was the beginning of our friendship with an outstanding American leader. No wonder he was so greatly loved and respected. It was a particular joy to confirm Barbara in a side chapel a few years later.

The installation of Russ was an impressive event. The church, as big as any English cathedral, was packed with members of the church and visitors. Everything signalled the beginning of an eventful, successful and happy ministry. Russ and Laura were clearly an ideal couple to take the work forward.

In the years that followed, our visits to St Martin's Houston and other places in the United States continued as we attempted to support the work of more traditionalist churches remaining in a deeply fractious national body. A discussion with Jim Baker III on one of our visits to Houston was extremely enlightening. Jim, besides being a highly able and successful politician and diplomat, had an analytical mind. He was in no doubt that the Episcopal Church, as a microcosm of the nation, expressed the polarised character of the nation between two types of political and social thought – one deeply traditional and the other open to new trends of belief and action. He argued that both went back to the revolutionary days of the nation. The Republican Party stood for the family and moral values, and the Democratic Party for a social-liberal platform of equality and LGBT rights. As we discussed these opposing trends neither of us took any comfort from the agreement that in society and in the Church a compromise would emerge. A battle for the soul of the Church would soon begin. At this point I asked Jim if he saw anything of value in the way the Church of England had dealt with the ordination of women in appointing "flying bishops" to allow differences to exist side by side. As a politician Jim Baker granted the value of this as a very important principle of gracious hospitality on the part of a dominant party. But he argued that this was anathema to the American spirit. Conquer or be conquered was, he contended, the spirit of the United States. I left our meeting very pessimistic about the chances of a happy outcome for traditionalists in The Episcopal Church.

I was not the only one with concerns. The Bishop of the diocese of Texas, Andrew Doyle, was also worried that the war over sexuality would dominate mission for years to come. The matter had to be addressed. He approached Jim at the James A Baker III Institute for Public Policy and meetings led to a Baker-Doyle proposal that allowed individual clergy, after conversation with his or her parish, to decide whether or not to bless homosexual unions. Russ was very much part of this conversation. The report, known as *Unity In Mission*, was a well-meaning attempt to heal the divisions that were undoubtedly hindering the work of the Church. This document, which has become very much part of the policy of the diocese, owes so much to the three men mentioned but especially to Jim Baker's immense ability, drawn from his huge political success in the Middle East and elsewhere, to overcome division. Although this document has been criticised, in Russ's words, "It has really proven to be a success. We no longer talk about issues around sexuality at diocesan meetings because this document actually reaffirms the ability of people to hold traditional or more progressive views without dividing the church."

Nonetheless, as in Britain and elsewhere, progress has been patchy in the States. The increasing liberalisation of the Church has given way to a harsh intolerance whereby conservative bishops and clergy were forced out of office. It seems that there is truth in the saying that "there is none so dogmatic as a dogmatic liberal". An illustration later was in the diocese of Albany where Bishop Bill Love, a greatly respected and devoted bishop, was forced from office because of his commitment to traditional marriage and opposition to same-sex unions. A church court ruled that he had violated his ordination vows and canon law when he banned same-sex marriages in his diocese. Bill resigned at Easter 2021. I with many others grieved that a noble, faithful and honourable ministry ended in such a way. Where do I find the way of Christ, I wondered to myself, in such an action? Have we now reached a point where "generous disagreement" cannot chart the way ahead? This applies as much to conservatives as liberals because the former can be as intransigent and difficult as the latter.

In my active period as Archbishop there was one province of the Anglican Communion that I longed to visit but the political situation made it impossible. The longed-for visit was to Myanmar, or Burma as it used to be called. The church in Dagenham supported missionaries to Burma and their tales had fascinated me. Among the first missionaries to that colourful country was the American Congregational, Adoniram Judson, and his wife Ann. He later rejected Congregationalism and became a Baptist, hence the very strong Baptist Church in Myanmar. A story was told about when he was on trial for preaching the faith. On his way to the court someone mocked him in English: "How great are the prospects of your mission, heretic?" Quick as a flash, Judson shouted back, "As great as the promises of God, my friend." Judson was released and set about baptising converts and establishing churches. Other Christian denominations were to follow with the Roman Catholic Church as the largest and the Anglican Church as a fairly small but vibrant body.

In 2011 Rowan Williams, Archbishop of Canterbury, asked if I would be happy to visit the Province on his behalf. As the Government of Myanmar was a military dictatorship the UK Government advised against official visits by the Archbishop – but there was nothing to stop a senior representative going in his stead. I was delighted to go to fulfil my ambition. It would be a short visit of fifteen days and, of course, I wanted Eileen to be part of it. But it was also essential for a staff member to accompany me and none better than my former adviser, Canon Roger Symon, who had been my Officer for the Anglican Communion when I served as Archbishop. Roger, an outstanding and wise colleague, went a few days ahead to set up the visit and prepare the way. In November 2011 the visit took place and turned out to be immensely interesting to us and, we were told later, beneficial to the Anglican Church in that land.

But it was not without its difficulties. On landing at Yangon on November 16th we went straight to our hotel to unpack and then to meet our hosts. Archbishop Stephen Than turned out to be a very young and very friendly archbishop of slight build. With him was Nan, his equally young and shy wife. Also present were Jeremy Hodges, Number One at the Embassy, representing the Ambassador, and Cynthia, the Mothers' Union representative. The briefing commenced with Jeremy giving an incisive and candid view of the Government and the difficulties from the British point of view. Although Jeremy saw no problem with me speaking frankly about the political and religious realities in my meetings with Government officials, the media and in public speeches, the strong advice was that care had to be taken for the sake of our hosts. The Archbishop, however, explained the dilemma of his church which suffered from its "double minority status", being a small church within a minority Christian population and a body whose members are largely drawn from minority ethnic groups perceived by the government as hostile. The consequences for him, as leader, and for his Church, was the possibility of hostile interrogation if overseas visitors met politicians or leaders of other faiths. Nevertheless, Stephen continued, he was happy for the programme to go ahead and he was happy for me to meet the pro-democracy leader, Aung San Suu Kyi. That cleared the air and enabled the programme to continue as planned.

A very practical problem hit us as soon as we arrived. No one had prepared us for the fact that it was impossible to draw money from international banks because of sanctions agreed by Western countries against the military junta. We had agreed to pay all our expenses, so that we would not be a burden to the Church, but it was clear that there was hardly any margin for error – or for the odd coffee. To make matters even more challenging, the Church had booked us into one of the most expensive hotels in the city, Hotel Park Royal, and had even made available to us an extra room which we did not need but had to pay for. Whilst we were there Eileen celebrated her 75th birthday but our inability to get money out of our account resulted in celebrating her birthday on November 21st with a cheap bottle of wine in our room.

The Church we found was in good heart with well-trained clergy, all of whom seemed to be young and very focused. The worship was exclusively Anglo-Catholic in style and done beautifully. The liturgy and practice had been offered to the Karen people by the first British missionaries, all High Church, and the tradition continues to this day.

But evangelism was out of question. Although I was asked to lead sessions on evangelism and church growth, the Church was forbidden to evangelise directly. All the work done by Christian churches in Myanmar was done among the Karen people and there were penalties for any abuse of the rule. My admiration grew for this greatly oppressed tribal body. The Karen people had always pressed for their own government because it was a distinct language and ethnic group with different traditions from the Bamar (Burman) majority people. While this limited the outreach of the Church, the emphasis that all churches placed on health care, provision for HIV sufferers and serving others meant that the Christian message was reaching many of the Bamar people.

A meeting took place with the Minister for Religions, Brigadier General Myint Maung, a friendly man of middle age with limited English. He was anxious to emphasise the importance of religious freedom and that, whilst Buddhism was the largest religious group, all faiths were free to flourish and that they get on very well. I knew that this view was highly contentious and, in certain parts of the country, quite wrong. There were often tensions between Muslims and Buddhists and between Christians and Buddhists; indeed it is clear that Christians and Muslims have been subjected to considerable violence. Buddhism claims to be an enlightened and peaceful religion and, on the whole, that had been my experience. This, indeed, was the claim of one of the most charismatic Buddhist leaders we had the privilege to meet: Dr Ashin Nyanissara, known as Sitagu Sayadaw, a man of seventy-three, internationally known for his humanitarian work and openness to other faiths. His English was good and it was reported to me that he was particularly fond of Christianity and its work among all people in need. Indeed, he was keen to tell me his story that when he was twenty-three and working near the Chinese border he had visited a Christian hospital (he may have needed treatment but that was not clear). He met the doctor and was struck by the way the hospital cared for all and placed no barrier before anyone needing help, including some Buddhist monks who were being treated. That very hospital, he said, became the model for his health care programme. The doctor was an American, Dr Gordon Seagrave, who I found out later had been a remarkable missionary doctor.

I was very impressed by this remarkable monk and his evident commitment to others. Sadly, however, some years later when the plight of the Rohingya Muslims became known to the world, Sitagu Sayadaw's attitude to Muslims became hostile, declaring a "call to arms against Muslims" and justifying violence by appeals to Buddhist sacred writings. Later events seemed to bear out the fact that even the most peaceful faith can become a force for evil when united with nationalism. But we were not to know that at the time and left the compound of this famous monk singing his praises.

On Sunday 20th November at the Ambassador's home we met Aung San Suu Kyi, 1991 Nobel Prize winner. The Ambassador, Andy Heyn, was an open friendly man who gave us a short briefing first about the woman that all Burmese people simply called "The Lady". He spoke of her commitment to the nation and her desire to be a healing force. He was frank that, for some people, especially the army and supporters of the government, she was a divisive figure and not all saw her as being part of the nation's future. But he personally had a huge regard for her and he advised us not to pull any punches in talking to her.

She was a slender, attractive woman who seemed completely at ease with herself and others. I began by quoting Archbishop Stephen Than's comment about her as "the nation's hope". She immediately responded by saying, "But there can be no hope without endeavour." Endeavour, she continued, means keeping one's eye on the goal and never surrendering one's principles and never giving in to hate. Then, turning to me, she asked me to define "hate". Put on the spot, I defined it as "an attitude of life that seeks to destroy and humiliate others". She seemed to approve my definition and went on to quote a young man who had told her that "someone who hates cannot see the good in the one he hates". We dug deeper into her present concerns. Was she hopeful for the future? She was still under house arrest; was she being treated well? She avoided the personal question and spoke frankly of the many young people who were political prisoners and treated brutally. "Compared to them," she said, "my imprisonment is genteel by comparison." However, she continued, "I have nightmares but unlike others I am not beaten up." Did she see democracy coming in her lifetime? She replied, "We return to the theme of hope. I am not getting any younger and I long for my people to be free."

Our discussion ranged over a wide variety of topics – the political, theological and personal. Without a prompt, she expressed her gratitude to the Christian faith when she was a child. Her grandfather had been a Christian convert and her mother a Christian believer also. She spoke with deep appreciation of her education in Church schools and, drawing attention to my surname, chuckled that at Delhi she was in "Carey House", named after the Baptist missionary, William Carey. On the subject of politics she was convinced that political change had to come from within the country. She personally was very uncomfortable with outside interference. It was necessary to work with the government, as far as possible – but the future lay with the young people. We found ourselves speaking once more about belief and what the values are that kept us all going. She saw a clear overlap of values between the Buddhist and Christian faiths. She drew a parallel between Myanmar and South Africa and she observed that apartheid had been defeated not by violence but through faith and love. She expressed her appreciation of the Truth and Reconciliation Commission in South Africa.

We had ninety minutes with this remarkable woman whose obvious charisma, commanding presence, intellectual precision, informal openness and friendliness, together with the occasional flashes of steel, made a profound impression on me and our small group.

Although some years later she did eventually lead the country to democracy, her inability to give hope to the Rohingya people, and indeed other minorities, reduced her popularity and disappointed her many friends and supporters. All of us indeed have clay feet and no doubt the pressure on her to conform to her nation's wishes must have been huge but her refusal to consider the inhuman plight of the Rohingya people will always mar her image as a peacemaker.

Much to my disappointment the content of our meeting with "The Lady" was not taken up by meetings with members of the Church or other leaders. Although I raised questions with significant people concerning her approach, many were not prepared to comment. "Heads down and let's get on with the work" was the unspoken attitude.

And there was no denying that the work of the Church was extremely encouraging. We visited three of the six dioceses: Yangon, Taungoo, and Myitkyina. There was always worship followed by traditional celebrations, presentations, dancing and speeches galore. I led two retreats, preached six times and gave one lecture to the Myanmar Institute of Theology. One could not help but admire the vitality of local ethnic traditions in which the life of the Church was embedded. There was an attractive simplicity in the vibrant colour and costumes which made a striking contrast to the celebrations of the liturgy which, though well attended and devout, retained the Englishness of the rites and hymnals inherited from English missionaries – all of whom had been sent home in 1964. I was greatly struck by the closeness of the fellowship among the members of the Church and the energy of the services they offered to society around them. It was expected that every member of the church should belong to one of four societies within the Church: Education (for children), AYPA (Anglican Young People's Association), Mothers' Union and Men's Association.

We spent one day at Holy Cross Seminary which had some sixty students who included fifteen or so young women. The average age of the seminarians was quite young but their level of commitment, engagement and intellectual vigour was very impressive. As I discussed with the students in an open session of Q and A, I noticed how great was the focus on service and making a serious difference to their communities. It was clearly the case that their focus was not nationalistic because, as a minority ethnic group, they were estranged from the predominantly Bamar and Buddhist nation. Remarkably, this did not lead them to become a withdrawn, small, self-serving entity – on the contrary, their commitment was to serve all around and those in need. I was told about the annual Monsoon Training Course which attracted forty or more young people who offered to go into areas ravaged by the annual monsoons to help rebuild the flimsy houses. The Mothers' Union, so central to Anglicanism wherever it is found, is also formidable and strong in Myanmar. The clinics and day care centres for children we visited in each of the three dioceses showed strong social commitment to vulnerable people.

Although brief, the visit gave us a valuable opportunity to see a province well led and faithful in its mission. I was able to present to the Archbishop of Canterbury a report of a small Church serving its own membership, and indeed the wider community, in the spirit of Christ. It had clear objectives and was well led. Its spirituality was deep, real and solid. Faced by an oppressive regime, the Church of the Province of Myanmar was responding well to the fire of persecution.

In the first part of my autobiography, *Know the Truth*, I wrote about the Rwanda genocide and how much it had affected Eileen and me. The murder of some 800,000 people of one tribal group by another simply did not make sense, and the fact that both Hutus and Tutsis were Christian made it all the more appalling. How could a nation so deeply influenced by Christianity commit such evil?

Eileen and I were among the first Westerners to visit the country after the genocide, when we were there in May 1995, and on our return home we made a commitment to follow up the visit with whatever help we could give. This took the form of supporting bishops and taking an active interest in the development of the country. It was not until 2014, the twentieth anniversary of the genocide, that an opportunity came to visit Rwanda once more. This time it was as Vice Presidents of Tearfund, a British evangelical aid charity which we had always supported and which has an extensive programme of aid in the country.

What a different visit this was. As we flew over the mountainous yet fertile land we could not but marvel at the beauty of Rwanda, a jewel at the heart of Africa. Yet the memory of our visit nineteen years earlier was very much alive in our thoughts. We had been traumatised by that visit and one memory particularly stuck out – a meeting in Kigali Cathedral where hundreds of Anglicans had gathered to welcome us but which, within minutes, had given way to accusations, condemnation and as close to violence as anything can get. In that consecrated building the Dean of the Cathedral, Alphonse Kahurije, a former student at Trinity Bristol – one of my students – had in 1994 been seized, taken away and murdered. His body was never found. As I looked down from the plane I thought of the photo at the top of the stairs in our house, a photo of four very young Rwandan children holding tools in tiny hands and clumsily trying to till a banana grove. Given to us by the Minister of the Interior on our first visit, it was a sign of hope for the future. Those very young children in the photo would now be in their twenties. Were they helping to build a more prosperous and peaceful land? It was my fervent hope and prayer that this was the case, and our second visit went a long way to show what a different land Rwanda was now.

We were taken to our hotel, the Garr Hotel, situated quite close to the centre and on a steep slope. As we drove there we could see that Rwanda had become more prosperous but we quickly discovered that, once we left the main roads, the side roads were slippery and unpleasant lanes, almost impossible to navigate when the rains came. However, we were not there as tourists but as people eager to find out how the Church was doing and especially the work of Tearfund. A sign that had greeted us as we left the airport was: "Kwibuka: Remember, Unite, Renew".

As we drove towards Ruhanga Church where the commemoration service was to take place, I wondered how anyone under the age of twenty-five could forget. On April 15th 1994 more than twenty-five thousand people seeking refuge at the church had been slaughtered. Now no longer used as a church for regular worship, it is the only Anglican church that has become a memorial site.

The commemoration service was long yet inspiring. We met

a young man called Eric who was thirteen when the killings commenced in and around the church. He told us his story. People had fled to the church believing that they would be safe there. The army arrived and started shooting. Eric's mother was killed and he was hidden by her body. Hours passed and then the killers returned to finish off those who could be heard groaning. They pretended to be rescuers and promised help. The survivors stood up only to find that they were in the hands of the murderers again. They were lined up in two groups. Those who had money could pay and get a quick death by shooting. The fate of those without money was to have their throat cut by machete. Eric, who had no money, stood behind a lady who gave the killers 1,000 Rwandan francs – about 90p. She was shot and, again, he was protected by the lady's body. Eric and his five-year-old sister were the only survivors from a family of seven.

We also met Dorothy Mukamurenzi, another survivor of the genocide. She had been just eleven and had lost her entire family in the massacre. Now a young attractive woman of thirty-one she stood before me in a long traditional dress wearing a clerical collar. She reminded me that I had preached in this church on my first visit in 1995 and she had been in the congregation. I was moved and amazed when she said that something I had said in my sermon turned her heart away from bitterness and revenge. She declared that my message was the start of her journey towards Christian service. How wonderful when a preacher hears such things. Now ordained, Dorothy was priest-in-charge of a parish at Ntunga where, among the many visible signs of a growing church, she was leading a course on "sexual violence", sponsored and assisted by Tearfund.

On the second day of our visit I was taken by the British High Commissioner to meet the President, Paul Kagame. I remembered our frank meeting nineteen years earlier when he had expressed his deep anger at the international community for allowing the genocide to happen. He had been intensely bitter towards the French who, he said, had colluded with the mainly Hutu-led army. He had expressed on that occasion his desire to switch his allegiance to the British Commonwealth. He had not changed much: tall, but more stooped than I remembered seeing him last, with a slightly imperious style. Eileen and I were given a warm welcome and a spirited exchange followed. We talked about the problems of the country. About the size of Wales, Rwanda has a population of twelve million. Land is very expensive and for ordinary people very difficult to obtain. The President explained that population growth is worrying with 50 per cent of the people under the age of twenty.

I asked about relationships between the two tribal groups, Tutsis and Hutus, and he replied that the country was completely unified with no lingering problems. The government consisted of both tribes and tension between the two sides was a thing of the past. Then the President launched into a bitter attack on colonialism. The Belgians, he argued, were responsible for the genocide because of their favouritism of Hutus and because they had created the conditions that led ineluctably to the 1994 killings. He became rather heated as he described the situation leading up to the massacre. As early as January 11th 1994 the commander of the UN force in Rwanda, Roméo Dallaire, had sent a worrying fax to his superiors in New York, called later the "genocide fax". Dallaire warned that he had received information on the existence of plans for massacres; militia in teams of forty had been set up and were capable of killing a thousand people in twenty minutes. The fax was set aside. As for the French, the President argued, they had continued delivering weapons to the regime until June. Rather than protecting the civilian population by their military intervention called "Operation Turquoise", the French forces even allowed the aggressors to retreat to Zaire, taking their weapons with them. It was largely France's betrayal of Rwanda that led to the President in 1994 applying to the British Commonwealth to become a member. He immediately made English the second language of the country.

We spoke about the role of the Church in the country. Relationships, said the President, are extremely good. All the churches are making major contributions to the harmony of the country and to social, educational and health programmes.

It was a refreshing meeting with one of Africa's outstanding leaders. It was followed by a debriefing with William Gelling, the High Commissioner, an absurdly young-looking man for such a major work. Aged thirty-three, he looked twenty-three but had all the qualities that we expect from the British diplomatic corps.

In his view, the decision in 1994 to replace French with English was a very bad mistake. Instead of launching it immediately the policy should have been introduced very gradually. The result was, William explained, that teachers who taught well in French could teach only basic English. This, he said, was holding up progress in education.

We drove away from the President's palace marvelling how, in the space of two decades, things had changed for the better. Yes, there were major problems but there was no question about the progress made, and the Church had shared in the peace and prosperity. In early 1995 Bishop Onesephore Rwaje, Dean of the House of Bishops – a godly and outstanding bishop – had seemed to be the only stable influence. Now Archbishop, Onesephore continues his remarkable ministry as a caring, relaxed leader with mission at the heart of all he does.

I led a two-day House of Bishops Retreat and found the bishops in good heart with a huge desire to be effective, missionary leaders. Our Western churches still assume that African leadership is poor with little learning. This is changing fast and we were agreeably surprised by the quality of the bishops and archdeacons. One of the bishops – Laurent – has a Ph.D. from an American university and the standard of the others is also high. On the other hand, the educational level of the clergy is generally pretty poor. We were told by a lay member of Tearfund that 85 per cent of the clergy had only attained primary education – that is, their education ended at around the age of twelve. Admittedly they went to college to study the Bible but their level of general education remained poor. The Church is facing this challenge and recruitment of better educated, younger men and women is going on. This should be seen as a reflection of the standard of education in the country generally. It is being addressed by the President but it is not helped by the fact that teachers are poorly paid.

We were struck by the way that women are coming through into the Church's ministry. Dorothy, mentioned earlier, is an example of a young single woman who is completely accepted by all her parishioners. We went into her simple home, which by Western standards seemed primitive – rough stone floor and furniture that looked homemade. Probably it was luxurious compared to that of ordinary people. Dorothy has three cows and a small garden that she tends. Most clergy have smallholdings to supplement very modest stipends. But her life was purposeful and her work as a clergy person respected.

We were delighted to see the extent of the links between Tearfund and the Anglican Church. Accompanied by Henrietta Blyth, a senior member of Tearfund, we saw some inspiring examples of the faith in action. A mushroom factory, micro-finance projects led and shaped by ordinary members of congregations, and other development projects that have given people hope and brought them out of poverty. Central to Tearfund's vision in Rwanda is the priority given to transforming the lives of people and this was echoed in every visit we made. When I teasingly asked what the link was between a mushroom and the gospel, I was told in no uncertain manner by one of the lay leaders that it was the gospel that led the people to consider investing in mushrooms. In the few years the factory was built – by the people themselves – it had blessed the lives of 1,300 people already and expansion was planned.

Our visit over, as we flew away from Kigali airport I found myself reflecting on our two visits to this beautiful land and my fundamental question rose to the surface: "How was it possible that genocide happened twenty years ago?" I thought of the terror it must have created, the families destroyed, machetes raised by ordinary people against their neighbours, teacher against teacher, doctor against doctor, perhaps even husband against wife. Madness. I thought of my former student Alphonse, Dean of Kigali Cathedral, murdered, probably by people he knew well and had trusted. Incomprehensible. And then I remembered that this same species, capable of such acts of terror, is also capable of love and tenderness, and of immense compassion and mercy. Finally my thoughts lingered on Dorothy, that young priest, full of promise and hope. Yes, I thought, in such young people and her generation lies Rwanda's future.

7

The Gift of Education

If a man empties his purse into his head, no man can take it away from him. An investment in knowledge always pays the best interest.

Benjamin Franklin

Benjamin Franklin, who uttered those words, knew all about the price of education. Perhaps one of the greatest of the Founding Fathers of the United States, he hardly had an education at all. As far as we know, he had two years of education at Boston Latin School but never graduated, and it appears that formal education ended for him when he was ten years of age. But what he lacked in schooling he more than made up for through his voracious reading and intellectual ability. From those uncertain beginnings, he went on to become a major figure in the American enlightenment as a scientist, philosopher, statesman and diplomat.

Education for me also was a highly desired objective. I left school at the age of fifteen and a half and left frustrated, because I felt that there was so much I wanted to know and accomplish. As I have written elsewhere, my conversion to the Christian faith two years later ignited my thirst for knowledge and drove me on in my

Christian and public life. However, the problem for those of us who have had to make our own way educationally is, by definition, the lack of guidance in education. We need formation and the skill and brilliance of others. As I have already described, I went on to success in education and then on to teaching itself, but my experience showed me that a nation that does not have an ambitious system of learning for all children fails in its care for the young and will suffer against the competition of other nations.

Like many others, in the early 1990s I became very interested in the views of a young and talented politician, Tony Blair, whose radical reinterpretation of socialism was stirring the young and worrying the Establishment. I met Tony several times prior to his selection as leader of the Labour Party. His predecessor, John Smith, was an outstanding politician whose premature death was a blow to our parliament, as it was to the Labour Party. It was a privilege to preach at his memorial service in Westminster Abbey. This gave me something of an entrée into the leadership of the Labour Party and I was impressed by their commitment to change and to the renewal of the nation. In truth, Tony Blair's "third way" lay in his success in bringing the Labour Party back into mainstream politics. I was able to sense the rivalry, and yet the genuine partnership, between the intense Gordon Brown and the more relaxed Tony Blair. It was not a surprise to many when in 1997 the Labour Party led by Blair swept to power and promised to be a reforming government which would put the interests of the people first. Among an impressive set of goals, education would be high on the agenda. In my meetings with Tony Blair his commitment to changing for the good the life chances of the poor and left-behind were aspirations that echoed my own, driven as they were by his Christian faith. His famous quote on education was in a pledge made at the Labour Party Conference in October 1996, seven months earlier: "Ask me for my three main priorities for government and I tell you: education, education and education." The sound-bite stuck, and critics of the Labour government would turn it against ministers remorselessly. Curiously, and I will return to this later, there was no searching analysis of what was meant by education. It was as if we had all the same idea of the ideology behind education – which is far from the reality.

Tony Blair's victory represented a crushing defeat for the Major government. The media had been very damning and cruel in its judgment of John Major's government and policies. My experience of the Prime Minister was that he was certainly not "grey" or as mediocre as some of his critics declared. John was a good Prime Minister of integrity, and did many noteworthy things. But the nation wanted change and, after nearly two decades of Thatcherism, decided to give the Labour Party under Tony Blair a chance to bring that change.

A man known to me from the earliest days of my appointment as Archbishop was Ewan Harper, a businessman. Indeed, Ewan became a close personal friend and our collaboration in many different fields was very beneficial. Ewan, a few years younger than me, was CEO of the United Church Schools Trust, a modest group of independent schools. The group originated in 1883 when a group of Church of England families shared concerns about girls' education which was being left behind by the emphasis upon the education of boys. A strong social philosophy thus motivated these parents to ensure that young women and girls had the same opportunities as young men. Although the group never succeeded in growing into a large federation of schools, what it lacked in size it more than made up for in a few highly successful schools. Among them were Surbiton High School for Girls, Guildford High School for Girls, Sunderland High School, Hampshire Collegiate School, Ashford School, Bournemouth Collegiate and Lincoln Minster. Ewan Harper, a man of remarkable vision, energy and drive, took over the group in 1990 and the following twenty years was a period of great expansion that I was fortunate enough to share.

Initially, there did not seem much room for expansion in the competitive world of private education. There appeared little chance that a tiny group of schools, founded upon independent education and Anglican principles, could make any impact on the national scene. Tony Blair provided that opportunity. What came as a shock to many Labour supporters was Blair's determination to bring together private business, independent education and state education in a partnership to bring excellent education within the reach of all children. To do this required someone with immense vision, energy and imagination and Andrew Adonis was the man for the moment. Andrew, who had come from a broken home and had been educated at Kingham Hill School, a Christian foundation, went on to become an academic at Oxford University and then a journalist at the *Financial Times*. Attracted by Adonis's charisma and passion for change, the new Prime Minister appointed him to be adviser at the No. 10 Policy Unit, with special responsibility for constitutional and educational matters.

Ewan started to contemplate the role of the independent sector in terms of the Academy programme. He met with his board and argued that as a group of Christian schools they must have a role in such a national initiative. Despite the beginning of United Church Schools Trust as a mission to bring Christian education to girls, Ewan felt that the social issue in the dying days of the 1990s was no longer a gender matter but the state of education and failing schools in poorer parts of the country, left behind by a strong economy. Ewan then started to re-imagine the moral intention of the Trust if they were presented with this issue in their day. He concluded that now was the time to bring his small independent sector of schools directly into state education.

Then a woman friend of Ewan Harper's, who also knew Andrew Adonis well, mentioned to Adonis at a dinner party that Ewan had strong and exciting ideas that he needed to hear. The two men met at No. 10 and Adonis informed Ewan that he was very committed to creating a new form of school in the public sector, asking him, "Are you willing and able to take on the building and management of a City Academy?"

The question put Ewan on the spot but, as CEO, he could not answer immediately without the support of his board, even though his instinct was to accept at once. The board met, under the leadership of Lady Prior, wife of Jim Prior, Secretary of State for Employment in Margaret Thatcher's government. Understandably, the board was cautious for some obvious reasons. It had just commenced a programme for the merger of some smaller schools. To add to the challenge, it soon became clear that anyone who wished to join the Academy programme had to contribute two million pounds per school.

Ewan then came to see me. For some time we had been discussing the chairmanship of the board. Jane Prior had offered her resignation on health grounds and I was being sought to take over on my retirement as Archbishop. However, chairing a group of what seemed to me to be "privileged", "middle-class" schools did not appear a worthwhile pursuit after an active life of service in the community. This, however, was a completely different and exciting project – to fuse independent education with state education had great social possibilities with wide-ranging implications. It did not take me long to agree and so I became President of United Church Schools Trust and was immediately pitched into a new and exciting work.

As I was chairing the board our first task was to give Ewan authority to negotiate with Andrew Adonis to establish our first Academy, with the objective of raising two million pounds towards the total costs. The school was the Henry Thornton School, just east of Clapham Common, in the district of Lambeth. Once a successful grammar school, it had fallen on hard times. It had been merged with a failing school and it was well on the path to becoming a "failed" school in its own right.

Once retired, I began the process of getting Ewan Harper's remarkable work in the Church and education recognised and I was delighted when a knighthood was conferred on him for all he had achieved. The Prime Minister was pleased to identify with this request believing that Ewan was essential to the growth of the Academy programme and had much to give.

The board over which I presided from 2003 was formidable and included people of outstanding ability such as Air Chief Marshall Sir Michael Graydon, former fighter pilot and head of the RAF;

Stephen Brandon, lawyer; John Beardwell; David Barnes; and Professor Mike Clark of Southampton University among others. I agreed that I would assist in fundraising for the Academies, in addition to the ongoing work of our existing schools. We decided to approach a Japanese gentleman, Dr Haruhisa Handa, whom I knew from contact through the Parliament for Religion and Peace. Dr Handa was, and is, an extraordinary man. Combining his calling as a Shinto priest with commercial work in the travel business, he developed quite staggering initiatives in humanitarian work. I knew that he had founded over a hundred schools in China as well as schools in Albania and elsewhere. He went on to establish an orphanage, university and hospital in Cambodia.

Ewan and I invited Dr Handa to dinner in the House of Lords. He agreed then and there to offer one million dollars to Lambeth Academy. It was a wonderful gesture from an old Eastern faith to a school with Christian principles. But that gift not only encouraged others to give; it also galvanised our desire to make a real commitment to the Academy programme.

In the meantime, I was asked to become a Patron of the Academy Sponsors Trust, along with Lord Levy and Lord Harris. Included in our responsibility as Patrons was support for the Director, Mrs Rona Kiley, a lady of immense energy and wisdom.

No sooner had we found the seed money for the first school than Andrew Adonis knocked at our door with a second and possibly more demanding challenge – to take over a school at Moss Side, Manchester, one of the very worst inner-city areas in the country, an area which the police were reluctant to patrol at night. There were two secondary schools in the district, Trinity School, a Church of England school, and Ducie High School, both struggling to be effective. Ducie High School was performing so badly that it was threatened with closure. Andrew Adonis had approached several potential sponsors but each one had turned it down as a "basket case" and too much of a reputational risk to consider further. It probably was total madness to take over this Ducie High School, which long ago had been a beacon of excellence but had gradually deteriorated to become a "sink" school, with one of the worst exam records in the UK. Lord Adonis would describe it later as "the most gang-infested comprehensive school in the country". So Manchester Academy became our second school, presenting us with serious challenges to do something dramatic, even exceptional, in education by reversing the calamitous record of failed education and failed children.

But education is not merely about what goes on in classrooms; it is also about what is happening in the family and the community. In the case of Manchester, the children were hopelessly handicapped by poor conditions in so many ways: inadequate housing, parents with no aspirations for their children, and communities saturated by drugs, violence and child pregnancy.

It was hard enough raising money for the Academy programme and, at the same time, seeking to improve the quality of education, but it was a real shock to discover that we were also the centre of a political battle. The Academy programme was based on the idea of the school supported by a sponsor or sponsors, set in the community and freed from the local authority. This was anathema to local authorities who, until then, had had control of schools, including appointments and buildings as well as budgets and salaries. The Academy programme challenged this autonomy, giving authority and independence to schools, which dismayed many local councils. But councils were not the only ones incensed: the Church of England, for a time, was opposed. An example of this was the opposition we faced when Lambeth Academy began. Ewan Harper had a difficult meeting with the Bishop of Southwark who challenged the authority of the United Church Schools Trust to place an Academy in its diocese without permission – in spite of the two archbishops being Patrons of the Trust. This "hostility" appeared in some other dioceses in the next few years and only disappeared when John Hall, later to become Dean of Westminster Abbey, was appointed Chief Education Officer for the Church of England in 2002. John used that senior and historic office to build bridges. He was a breath of hope. The Church of England later became a prominent and welcome sponsor of Academies particularly under

Gordon Brown, when sponsors were no longer expected to raise money for their role. That, unfortunately, was not the position during the Blair years when we had to raise some eighteen million pounds.

The period from 2002 to 2006 proved to be a challenging time as we set targets to raise large sums of money and, at the same time, received further requests to set up Academies in challenging areas: Stockport, Barnsley, Northampton, Paddington, Salford, Swindon, Walthamstow and two schools in Sheffield. During the following years many other schools approached the government to become Academies and, in turn, the government asked us to take some of them on.

But something had to be done about the title of our organisation, as United Church Schools Trust did not fit well with our new role. We decided that the company had to be separated into two distinct groups: United Church Schools Trust, comprising our ten or so independent, fee-paying schools, and the Academy programme which we entitled United Learning. Ironically, it was not long before United Learning became the larger of the two bodies.

Many lessons were learned in the early days of promoting the Academy programme. One of the most critical focused narrowly on a widespread suspicion that the academisation of education was merely a political subterfuge to privatise education and substitute a business model for professional educators. Of course, nothing could be further from the truth but, in fairness, we could understand the reason for this suspicion. It had to do with a view of education as a separate and distinct profession. The involvement of successful business and local community was greeted with horror in many parts of the country. But this, in turn, was an elitist reaction – as if schools had nothing to learn from success in life and business. Allied to such a suspicion was another factor. A marked feature of British life is our tendency to encourage "binary" opposites: good versus evil, dark versus light. The aggressive businesslike competition that many feared would result (the negative side) was seen as being in opposition to the country's comprehensive school system (the positive side). Thus it was imperative to show that Academies were not in opposition to excellent education, in whatever system it existed, but against poor education per se. The clear evidence was that in many parts of the country children were the victims of indifferent education, at best, and shockingly poor education at worst. Indeed, a government document set out the vision for the Academy programme: "To put a good school on the doorstep of the poorest communities."

As we increased our numbers of schools and learned from the experience, several factors came into prominence. The most important was that excellent education started at the top of the organisation, and that is where reform had to begin. Manchester Academy was a case in point. Our first Principal was Kathy August, an experienced educationalist with headships in northern schools. There was no reason for her to show any interest in this poor school in Moss Side, with massive social problems and no Sixth Form. But it was the school's endemic record of failure that actually interested Kathy. She felt an immediate professional challenge in the invitation we presented to her, and she was prepared to give it her all. I recall the opening of the new building in 2006 where, with TV cameras present and the Mayor and leaders of the city as guests, the children presented a programme. A boy of sixteen had promised to sing but at the last moment suffered from stage fright. Kathy tried to coax him to sing his song but to no avail. Then, movingly, she stood alongside him and sang the song, so that he could regain his courage and take over. We were all touched by her compassion and awareness. It was not only the sight of a dedicated teacher coaxing a nervous student to take part, but it also raised for me the question: how many male teachers would have the courage and risk scoffing to sing along with a student?

As our group of schools expanded, so as a board we increasingly realised the importance of appointing head teachers of outstanding ability and vision. Without such qualities our new schools, into which we poured such hopes as well as money, would surely fail. Such teachers were not as plentiful as we would have liked. Ewan and his senior team met some disappointments as well as successes in finding outstanding individuals. Not only did the heads have to have great teaching qualifications but they had to have a love of children and a vocation to bring the best out in children who, in many cases, society had already written off. And "vocation" was the key word. It was a word frequently used in times past for the teaching profession but had faded away. At United Learning we recovered it, without using the word all that often. I saw it in the long hours that our outstanding senior teachers worked. I saw it in the way they motivated younger teachers. I saw it in their enthusiasm for their schools and their pride in their children when they excelled.

Paddington Academy was also a school we rated as having great potential. In 2006 the government asked us to take over North Westminster Community School which was judged by Ofsted as having "standards that remain low and achievements that are inadequate". Less than 25 per cent left school with five A-C grades at GCSE. Those of us on the board were in no doubt of the challenge that Ewan and his senior team were presented with. The period between 2006 and 2010 was a period of profound shake-up in the school and which showed in indifferent academic success. The spotlight was on the school, with some outside the Academy network willing the school to fail. But the opposite happened. In 2010 Paddington Academy became the second most improved academy in England. In 2011 it received the third highest number of students receiving five or more A-C grade GCSEs in Westminster. In that year the Academy was judged "outstanding" by Ofsted. This achievement coincided with the arrival of our second head teacher, Olli Tomlinson, a bright, young woman with an engaging personality and fresh approach. Under Olli the Academy has progressed in a dazzling fashion, with all top universities within reach of able students.

Paddington and Manchester Academies, however, were not the only models for our schools springing up and down the country. A framework was emerging whereby our expectations were being met, based upon fairly "ordinary" criteria: an emphasis upon "routines" and zero tolerance for bad behaviour, lateness and rudeness. There was an expectation that every child would do her or his best and there was hatred of mediocrity. The underlying philosophy, based upon a Christian ethic, was love of children which preceded all other motivations. Our intense desire to drive up standards was expressed in our motto which was hammered out in a number of board meetings that I chaired: "The Best in Everyone". Under Kathy's leadership, within five years Manchester Academy gained an "outstanding" commendation from Ofsted, and also secured some very high "value added" scores which showed that pupils from disadvantaged homes could perform as well, if not better, than their more advantaged peers.

Although the head teacher set the standard, the rest of the staff were also critical to the success of education in our schools. The zero tolerance we expected from children was an expectation applied to teachers as well. We had to tackle absenteeism and slackness and, sometimes, very poor teaching. The head was expected to move teachers out if they could not live with our demands. I saw this in an appalling way a few years later when we were in the process of taking over a failing school in Walthamstow. I shared horrified looks with Ewan Harper as the head teacher thanked the teachers for turning up that morning.

No school can ever be separated from the culture of the community in which it is set and is often significantly influenced by it. Manchester Academy was particularly affected by the lawlessness and drug-related crimes of Moss Side. Our fledgling new Academy was rocked when in September 2006 a fourteen-year-old pupil was shot four times whilst out cycling with friends. The innocent victim of gang violence, Jesse James, was killed instantly. Kathy August had to demonstrate all her skill as an outstanding head to bring some form of healing to the devastated community.

One of the finest moments for Manchester Academy came in 2011 when riots hit the city. Initially, the violence started in Tottenham with the shooting of a drug dealer, Mark Duggan. Within a few days, violence took the form of attacks on police but soon escalated to widespread looting. In Manchester and Salford thousands of youths ransacked shops, attacked police and torched cars. A hundred and thirteen were arrested.

Manchester Academy was situated at the centre of the violence, and the board believed that we had a civic responsibility to keep our children out of the violence. Jesse's senseless death five years earlier was a vivid reminder that we had every reason to be vigilant. One of the local committee of the Academy was the owner of "Richer Sounds", a shop that specialised in TVs and up-market luxury products, and had several of his shops looted, but he was among those who helped the school keep the children safe both in school and at home. As a result of working with the parents we found that not one of our children engaged in the riots, a fact applauded by the police. It showed that our policy – that education affected every aspect of life – was paying off in the school itself and in the wider community.

As our schools expanded and we were in a position to consider critically our successes, certain factors leapt to our attention. The first was a serious examination of what we meant by education. As mentioned at the beginning of this chapter, the assumption was we were all agreed about the aim of education, which was largely concerned with passing examinations and making young people worthy citizens. I was delighted to be on a board that was prepared to examine that superficial conclusion closely and to dig deeper into the task before us. Professor Mike Clark was a particular inspiration in this endeavour and his innovative work at Southampton University was of great significance. Although Mike was not motivated, as far as I could tell, by a Christian philosophy of education, he respected the enormous contribution that Christianity had given and continues to give to schools in Britain. He agreed with me that to see education as a "tool", by which we acquire knowledge in order to reach a certain level of competence for life, is a severe truncation of education as we have come to understand it. John Henry Newman's renowned study, *The Idea of a University*, rejected any reduction of education to it being a mere tool. For

Newman education, from its Latin root, means "leading out" to knowing, understanding, comprehending. Essentially, then, in my analysis of its meaning, education is curiosity, pursuing knowledge for its own sake. With Newman I saw education as being far more than acquiring information in order to equip a person for a career. If it did not include shaping of a whole personality of a cultivated woman or man, it fell short of its potential grandeur. Of course, as a Christian, all this was inseparable from moral and spiritual education. I was delighted that Mike and indeed all the trustees shared this larger view of what we were doing together.

A second principle was aspiration. We could not avoid the fact that the difference between working-class British children, particularly boys, and immigrant children was seen in their desire or lack of it to break out of the cycle of poverty. At Manchester Academy we saw the aspirations of Somali children, particularly girls, as they mastered English with ease and showed prowess in all subjects. Such devotion to learning evoked our respect and admiration. This, sadly, was such a sharp contrast with the two Academies set up in Sheffield – Sheffield Park and Sheffield Springs. The schools we took over were terrible indictments of a failed education system. Sheffield Springs was known for its broken windows and the bills for their repair were colossal and relentless. Replacing such a rundown building by a modern, first-class school with up-to-date facilities, we wondered if our academy would be treated differently. But it was. It seemed as if the neighbourhood respected the fact that they were being treated as responsible citizens and, therefore, were keen to protect their school buildings. Of central importance, however, was not the physical buildings but the quality of what was going on in them. We found in such working-class areas, not only lack of aspiration, but also a complete lack of interest on the part of parents. In a number of our schools we tried after-school activities for parents to awaken their interest in their children's work. In some cases this paid off as parents were inspired to do more for their children but, by and large, even those who were willing to give up time soon found the commitment too hard. There were also other factors at work. In the majority of cases we found that children did not have the luxury of a quiet room at home to do homework. There was huge competition for space from their siblings and demands by parents for odd jobs to be done – without adding to this the temptation of the all-enticing TV or games console in the corner. But slowly standards began to rise and Ofsted was starting to recognise the huge efforts the pupils were making at our Sheffield schools. In other working-class areas we were hitting the same problems and also beginning to see results from the work of dedicated teachers and aspiring pupils. We were so encouraged when at Stockport Academy one girl was awarded a place at Trinity Hall, Cambridge, to read Natural Sciences. The impact on the school and neighbourhood was remarkable as it sent out a signal, "If one person can do it, why not more, why not – me?"

For a very long time as President of the United Church Schools Trust I was pondering about a most troubling issue – how to deepen the Christian character of our schools. This was Ewan Harper's desire as well. Both of us wanted the moral fibre of the Christian faith to penetrate the life of our schools. As a former Archbishop I was only too aware of the challenge facing Church schools having meaningful assemblies and a true Christian identity. It was very clear from our independent schools that it was far from easy. Indeed, to be frank, we had been merely playing at it; assemblies were largely times at the beginning of the school day for notices to be given. It was only on special occasions that a hymn might be sung and a talk given. If, then, we were finding challenges in our established schools, what were our hopes in our Academies?

However, there was a presentational problem that we had no awareness of until rumours reached us that United Learning was considered a "deeply evangelical" organisation and that we were on a mission of conversion. How this silly perception came about we had no idea, although it might have been influenced by my reputation as Archbishop. We had to make it clear that our goal was education, not conversion, and we were not in the business, either, of employing practising Christians only. We were greedy for the best of teachers, who loved children. If teachers combined this with a Christian faith, then that was all to the good.

So the question remained: "How may our Christian legacy be a reality in our new schools?" We decided that all new-builds should have a room set aside for faith communities to meet, and in a number of cases the outcomes were successful. In both Manchester and Sheffield Park Academies, Muslim children could undertake ritual Islamic washing with prayers led by local imams. However, this created a challenge when the imam wanted to use Arabic. Confronting this problem, Kathy and her senior team had to establish a clear rule that English was the only language to be spoken. This was a must because seventy-one languages were spoken by the school's children. A later Principal, Dr Antony Edkins, insisted that a member of staff be present to hear what was said. Initially, this met with opposition until the Muslim students understood that the reason was not to monitor the essence of the talk but to support children in their development.

Sadly, I have to admit that during my time as President, we never did manage to raise the profile of the Christian faith, and I had to accept that across the network of Academies it largely depended upon the Principal and his or her staff. What we did see, however, was that from the strong Christian origins of our organisation sprang a commitment for excellence in each child and that remains a wonderful gift from the past to schools today.

There was an equally important issue that troubled me from the day I became President. I found myself supporting independent schools, even though my own background was in the state sector. Indeed, I had an ambivalent relationship to independent education which was, of course, regulated by the wealth of parents. It was such an eye-opener to see the excellence of the independent schools in our group. I could not deny that it was the inspiration of independent education that launched United Learning and, without it, United Learning would not have seen life. Visits to Guildford High School and our other historic schools revealed dedicated teachers, aspiring children, small class sizes, and the most wonderful facilities. As a board, our job was to support our schools and, if they needed a swimming pool or new playground, it was our role to provide them with anything which helped to improve the physical or mental health of our youngsters. The same went for the teaching staff. Because we were able to remunerate teaching staff at a more ambitious level, we had no difficulty attracting excellent teachers.

Whilst the introduction of Academies helped to redress somewhat the balance in the education we were providing, the board were thrown into a position where we could see the sharp differences between state and independent education. We could see how difficult it was to recruit good teachers in very challenging neighbourhoods where student behaviour was bad and support from parents was non-existent.

This, however, provided us with a real opportunity to work with teachers across the group and the independent schools were enthusiastic and helpful. With modern technology, maths teaching could be shared without a teacher leaving a classroom. On other occasions, depending upon distance, teachers from our more affluent independent schools could visit United Learning schools. Academic excellence increased as a consequence.

A deeper moral issue affected me keenly. Now presiding over state independent schools I found myself wrestling with a national matter of great importance. It seemed very wrong that our national educational system was so elitist. For two centuries a small number of "public" schools have dominated English education leading to a form of apartheid based on wealth and leading also to assumptions of entitlement. Robert Verkaik's book, *Posh Boys: How English Public Schools Ruin Britain* (2018),[15] is a stinging attack on the unfairness of this dominance and the "toxification" of education. Verkaik attacks what he calls "the blatant theft of education" as the altruistic and philanthropic intentions of the original founders ended up in the pockets of the rich. Intended at the start to benefit the poor, the poor can no longer afford them. It is startling to discover that the prestigious Eton College, founded by King Henry VI as a charity school to provide free education for seventy poor boys, is now one of the most expensive schools, charging nearly £50,000 annually per pupil. As a visitor to the college on a number of occasions I have nothing but admiration for the quality of its work and its desire to give boys the best start in life it can offer. Verkaik's desire is for the slow and painless euthanasia of the private sector whereby its privileges are slowly whittled away. Personally, I cannot see this happening. Having seen the excellence of public school education my yearning is for this to be shared and for all public schools to be compelled to include poorer students in a more radical and costly way.

Indeed, the nation should be deeply ashamed that education is so unequal, with such little attention being given to the poverty of opportunities offered to working-class children. Tony Blair, a public school boy himself, was clear-sighted enough to see the urgency of the problem and to address it determinedly. From the perspective of the United Church Schools Trust I could see that the life chances of the vast majority of children were affected by the bias toward private education. It showed up in the struggle that United Learning found in raising the standards in our Sixth Forms. Whereas in Guildford High School virtually every Sixth Form girl achieved several A grades at A level, it was a reason for great rejoicing if just a few in our Academies did so. But this was no different from the national average for state education. In 2018, 48 per cent of private school students achieved A grades. This was nearly double the national average of 26 per cent.

As a board we never discussed this national issue of the disparity between independent and state education, but simply took it as a fact that we could not deal with such a far-reaching problem. This made some of us very uneasy. Even though the majority of the board had benefited from private education – I was certainly in a minority – at least we could take some pride in being among the very few independent networks that was actually doing something practical about it. We were reaching out into the state sector, and making a huge effort to improve the life skills and education of those from poorer backgrounds.

The splendid words of Ernest Bevan, former Labour Minister, seem to resonate with respect to this concern. In the war years he often mourned the lack of aspiration of Welsh working-class people.

He said: "The trouble with my people is the poverty of their desire."

The same could be said about the issue of schooling. Whereas it is a not unreasonable fact of life that those with enough money are free to purchase expensive cars, luxurious homes and enviable holidays, education is not just another material thing. Education is fundamental to what kind of nation we are, and the kind of people we want our children to be. I can see that our national predilection will always be to give freedom of choice to parents so that they can select for their children the type of schooling that will benefit them. We can all understand that. But in an unequal society, we have to live with the unhappy consequences of this. It affects every aspect of our national life: politics, the media, civil service and, until recent times, the Church. As long as private education exists with such massive advantages, the vast majority of children will suffer from the inequality. This is unfinished business, as far as the United Kingdom is concerned, which must be addressed at some point in the future.

Sir Ewan Harper retired from his post as Chief Executive in 2011 after nearly twenty-five years of outstanding leadership which touched the life chances of countless children. He was followed by another distinguished public servant in the form of Mr John Coles, from the Department of Education. John went on to build upon Ewan's strong foundations.

I resigned from the Presidencies of United Learning and United Church Schools Trust in 2017 feeling what an immense privilege it had been to have played a small part in driving up the life chances of so many children. It had also been an immense privilege working with Ewan Harper and his gifted colleagues, from whom I gained so much. I had taken on that role desiring that children should have a better start to their education than I had had. I was deeply thankful to have been given the opportunity to achieve that. When I retired, United Learning was a group of over fifty Academies. Since then it has grown to well over sixty. It remains committed to both independent and state education. I think Benjamin Franklin would have approved.

8

Radical Change of Heart

It takes courage to grow up and become who you really are.

E.E. Cummings

The story is told of John Maynard Keynes, one of the most influential economists of the twentieth century, that when some of his detractors complained that the opinions he expressed tended to change over the years, he replied: "When the facts change, I change my mind. What do you do, sir?"

That, for me, is how we all grow as human beings. To re-think one's position on a given subject and to take a different stance is a fairly normal occurrence. However, such an action for a public figure associated with an organisation that has an explicit message on a given subject may have serious consequences. The Church of England, along with all mainstream Christian churches, has taken a clear and determined view on euthanasia and assisted dying. The difference between the two is that euthanasia refers to the situation when someone else – usually a doctor – directly ends another person's life to relieve their suffering, while assisted dying is when the sick person takes his or her own life but with assistance from another.

I naturally identified with the traditional view that the sanctity of human life forbade the taking of that life in any form. For years I had been opposed to any alteration of the official doctrines of the churches on not encouraging people to commit suicide. But this was to change as I went deeper into the subject.

On May 12th 2006 Lord Joffe introduced a bill into the House of Lords entitled "Assisted Dying For the Terminally Ill". On the face of it Joel Joffe and I had little in common. He was a Jewish atheist and humanist, but I got to like this attractive and compassionate man. We enjoyed a number of conversations that united us in our concerns for peace in the Middle East and our common friendship with Nelson Mandela.

Lord Joffe said in his opening remarks:

> The current law has the following defects. It results in unnecessary suffering by a significant number of terminally ill patients who are denied the right to end their suffering by ending their lives and the right, as they see it, to die with dignity. It is ignored by some caring doctors who, from time to time, moved by compassion, accede to persistent requests by suffering patients to end their lives. That results in grave risks to those doctors' careers, reputations and possibly freedom. It is also ignored by loved ones who face a terrible emotional burden when helping with such a request. It places patients at risk of making spontaneous and ill-formed decisions to end their lives. It influences patients with progressive physical diseases to end their lives earlier than they need to.

There was much in his speech that I identified with, but I felt that his goal of legalising assisted dying for the terminally ill was dangerous and unjustified by the facts.

I offered this point:

> I am against this bill for many reasons – not least
> because its effects would alter the precious relationship
> between doctors and patients and assisted suicides
> could, before a few years are out, be treated as casually
> as abortion is treated today. The BMA in its most
> recent pronouncement on this bill remarked that the
> unevenness of good quality palliative care is a matter
> of extreme concern to doctors.

Lord Joffe's bill was subsequently defeated but it was obvious
from wide support for Lord Joffe's concerns that the issue was not
going to recede from view.

That debate left me uneasy and troubled because the *ex cathedra*
pronouncements that I and other public figures were trumpeting
were not, in fact, justified by the facts. We were all aware that the
Bible contributes nothing directly to this debate. There was nothing
in Holy Writ, or in two thousand years of Christian teaching, that
bore directly on this modern problem, largely created by the success
of modern science and improved health care. Furthermore, I began
to see that statements like human beings are "made in the image and
likeness of God", that life is "sacred", that "thou shalt not kill", were
too broad as principles to be very relevant to the issue.

So I found myself in the uncomfortable position that, although
I took the Bible very seriously as the main authority for my life, I
was beginning to waver in my conviction that to assist others to end
their lives in peace was always wrong.

As I mentioned earlier, to break ranks from my Church and the
entire Christian tradition on this matter was a momentous step. I felt
I had to check this out with people I trusted. I sought the wisdom
of Rabbi Jonathan Romain, a greatly respected Jewish leader within
the liberal tradition of Judaism. Jonathan was already known as
someone convinced of the rightness of assisted dying in strictly
agreed and controlled circumstances. His views were valuable and

reassured me that my change of mind was well grounded. Jonathan pointed me towards a book by prominent theologian Professor Paul Badham entitled, *Is There a Christian Case for Assisted Dying?* Professor Badham's exploration of the theological and ethical issues convinced me that my thinking was along the right lines. In his introduction to the book, Paul Badham quoted Hans Küng: "Precisely because I am convinced that another new life is intended for me, as a Christian I see myself given freedom by God to have a say in my dying, a say about the nature and time of my death."[16]

It was the terrible experience of Tony Nicklinson, a man of fifty-eight, who, after having a stroke on a business trip in Athens in 2005, developed locked-in syndrome that finally convinced me in my change of view. Locked-in syndrome is a rare and horrifying neurological disorder characterised by complete paralysis of all voluntary muscles, except for the eyes. Up to that point a very fit man, a former rugby player and sky-diver, Nicklinson found himself totally paralysed with no ability to move other than his head and eyes. He had excellent medical support but was told that his condition was irreversible. For the next seven years he found himself incapable of moving, unable to speak, wash himself, go to the toilet or clean his teeth. Communication with his wife and family was through a computerised system that allowed him to write messages by blinking his eyes. In 2012 Mr Nicklinson commenced legal proceedings to end his life. His argument was that the current law was incompatible with his human rights. The High Court, although moved and sympathetic to his terrible predicament, refused to grant his wish and the petition went on to the Supreme Court. Again his request was refused on the basis that to seek assistance to die was incompatible with current law and only Parliament had the right to alter the law.

At this point everything came to a head. I was deeply shocked for Tony Nicklinson and deeply outraged for what appeared to be our callousness and neglect for the suffering and feelings of a fellow human being. Why is it, I found myself asking, that a terminally ill person may ask for a machine to be turned off and thus die, but cannot get medical assistance to die peacefully? A desperately sad Tony Nicklinson then refused food and drink and died a few days later.

The miseries experienced by Tony Nicklinson became the catalyst for my intervention on the other side of this debate. However, another motive also played its part in my change of mind. For some time I had been troubled that the deep conservatism of the churches held back the mission of Christianity. I found myself asking, "Why are we always against change?" Since 1633, when Galileo Galilei faced the Inquisition to answer for his assertion that the earth revolves around the sun, there have been clear differences between the approach of the Church to scientific thought and the views of scientists. Whether it was the medieval churches' objection to dissecting dead bodies for research, or modern objections to contraception, or to stem cell research, or mitochondrial donation, the churches always seemed to be ceding ground reluctantly, instead of being a welcoming partner in the goal of relieving distress and disease. Once more, it seemed to me that my Church was putting dogma before the needs of people.

In 2014, having consulted with doctors, pain specialists, theologians and friends, I finally decided to go public with my change of heart. In an article for the *Daily Mail*, and with considerable trepidation I wrote that I intended to support legislation tabled by the Labour peer Lord Falconer, former Lord Chancellor, to legalise assisted dying for the terminally ill in England and Wales. Under that bill, which was going to be considered the following week in the House of Lords, mentally capable adults with less than six months to live would be able to request help to die peacefully.

I was fully aware that this would astonish and indeed anger the leadership of the Church although, curiously, surveys had shown that the majority of Christian people were sympathetic to assisted dying.

The day before the article was published on Saturday, July 11th 2014, I felt that out of courtesy I should contact Justin Welby, the Archbishop of Canterbury, to alert him to my action. He returned my call within minutes and was clearly furious. He shouted down the phone: "I am here in York for General Synod. How dare you intervene in such an important matter!" I could not believe my ears that, without giving me an opportunity to explain the background, he should speak to me in such a belligerent manner. I told him that I was acting courteously by giving him fair warning of my intention to write but, I went on to say, that I was not going to be spoken to in such a rude manner. Justin calmed down and the rest of the conversation was civil, though strained. Later the Archbishop expressed his opposition to the Falconer Bill, arguing that to change the law could put vulnerable people under pressure to end their lives, so as "not to be a burden" and to legalise assisted dying would leave a "sword of Damocles" hanging over the heads of elderly people.

The most trenchant criticism of my stance was presented in the *Daily Telegraph* by Bishop Michael Nazir-Ali, a very good friend. Under the title "Lord Carey's Judgment on Assisted Dying is un-Christian", Bishop Nazir-Ali offered a powerful defence of the current law. Although he told me later that the title was not his, it did sum up the contents of the article. In it he states that "I am simply amazed at his arguments (or lack of them) in support of Lord Falconer's Bill", and later in the article I am accused of failing to "take account of what the Judaeo-Christian tradition teaches about the human person". I must say that there was much in the article that I agreed with – the Christian teaching on the value of the human person, the duty of care and the prohibition on killing, especially the elderly. But absent in the article was any recognition of the issues that have brought us to this point where the majority of our fellow citizens feel that the law MUST change. They, and now I, believe it must change to take into account the reality that there are many who are desperate to end their lives, because of acute pain, distress and sheer indignity. In talking to relatives of those who have taken the course of suicide I have noted that, alongside unbearable pain, other factors such as loss of independence and inability to control one's bodily functions have also played decisive roles in desiring death. Naturally, with Michael Nazir-Ali, I admire the wonderful work of the hospice movement and those involved in palliative care in our hospitals. But, as he recognises, good palliative care is not available everywhere and, in my opinion does not address the reasons why so many are demanding a change in the law. What, however, was missing in his article was any understanding of the reasons why people seek the help of a physician to die, or go to Zurich, or ask a friend or relative to help them pass away. Following the *Daily Mail* article I was shocked by many letters from people who recounted their experience of loved ones who sought to end their lives in peace. In very, very few cases had the experience been edifying; in most cases their journeys were traumatic, with acute suffering and distress marking their final days. Bishop Michael remains a good friend whom I admire greatly but, sadly, I did not find in his article any awareness of the incomprehensible pain, suffering and indignity that more than a few dying people experience.

My article attracted enormous attention and my mail bag was impossibly full. The reaction was very mixed. The vast majority of writers supported my action although there were many who were deeply saddened by my article. Some felt very let down by a man who, they thought, was a "Bible Christian", "man of faith", "an evangelical". Of course, such reproachful letters depressed me but my conscience was telling me that I had acted in the right way.

The following week the Falconer Bill was considered in Parliament and the interest in it throughout the world was great. Charles Falconer introduced it very well and the tone of the debate was civilised and courteous. There were a hundred and ten speakers and my contribution of four minutes came in the afternoon. I said: "My Lords... I regret enormously the shock that I have given friends, some in this House, who disagree with my conclusions [in the *Daily Mail* article] but how can I really repent of a decision that I believe more closely models and reflects God's mercy and love?" I went on to comment on the matter of pain:

> I have the greatest admiration for the work of our hospices, but even the best palliative care does not meet all needs. Dr Rajesh Munglani, a well-known

expert in pain management, writes that he frequently
sees cases of excruciating pain that are unresponsive
to powerful analgesic, which can be alleviated only by
very heavy sedation, to the point of unconsciousness.

In making this point I was quite aware that within a few feet of me
was sitting one of the most eminent palliative experts in the country,
Baroness Finlay. She and I had shared platforms in presenting our
concerns on assisted dying to health professionals and I knew that
she was very distressed by my change of heart. Our relationship
changed from being quite friendly and warm to being cool and
distant. I am sure that she was as saddened as I by that, but it shows
how deeply committed opinions may change our attitudes to others.
In her case she was acutely aware of her vulnerable patients and
wanted to protect them from abuse. I could certainly understand,
and indeed shared that point of view.

However, pain is a terrible reality to sufferers and in many cases
of advanced cancer blights the lives of those nearing the point of
death. It was in exploring the nature of pain for dying people that
I came across the name of Professor Rajesh Munglani. Now based
in Cambridge, Raj, as he likes to be called, is a remarkable man
who came as a boy from India with his Hindu parents. Through
exceptional ability and hard work he excelled at school and
university, reading medicine at Cambridge, and in time became
a leading expert in pain management. Raj and I had lunch in the
House of Lords and I picked his brains on the issue of pain at the
end of life. He explained to me that palliative care in the UK is
extremely professional and effective but unfortunately at least twice
a year most pain consultants are referred by hospices and hospitals
cases where patients experience unbearable pain that the most
powerful drugs fail to help. Raj said, "It is in this kind of situation
that comments 'to put someone out of their misery' and 'you
wouldn't let a dog suffer like that' originate." Fortunately, he told me,
we can help control the pain of many but there are clearly some we
cannot without significantly sedating them. Raj mentioned a case

of a patient with severe rectal pain which had defied palliative and pain medicine. When Raj had described this severe case in a forum where the matter of assisted dying was also being addressed, the various options were discussed. Among these options was the use of intrathecal phenol which, Raj pointed out, would have made the patient doubly incontinent and possibly paralyse him permanently. Someone deeply opposed to assisted dying said that the patient "should be made to have the treatment, even if he did not want to". This reminded me of an opinion that Professor Nigel Biggar offered that "there is no such thing as pain that cannot be relieved, in so far as permanent sedation can always be used as a last resort". Although Nigel Biggar is a very well-known theologian whose views are usually to be respected, I found myself questioning his certainty. Could it be right that, against the wishes of an individual, we should sedate her or him to the point of unconsciousness? Is the prolongation of life at all costs and whatever the indignity caused to a very ill person the way we should solve the problem, whether or not the person wants such treatment?

These questions raise in their turn one of the most fundamental questions in the issue of assisted dying: that of autonomy – whose life is it, anyway? For most of us autonomy is taken for granted. We live our lives believing that we are in control, and when we seek medical help such decisions as we have to make are probably guided by the relationship we have with our physician. If she advises a certain course of medication we are likely to take it. Sometimes, however, we might question the prescribed medication because of its side-effects and the physician will probably demur and change direction. Personal autonomy is widely valued and considered to underpin what it is to be an independent person with value and dignity. In medicine it is a critical principle and no one can give medical treatment to another without their consent. I saw this first-hand when one of my grandsons became eighteen. A boy with severe heart problems, he had reached an age when his mother could no longer decide for him; he had to make his own choices for his life and future. It was not an easy time for him or his mother.

She was worried that he might make the wrong decisions, that he might forget appointments, that his anger about his condition might lead him to neglect himself. As it happened, he was sensible and came through the crisis very well but she was right to worry. The principle of autonomy limits the extent that relations, doctors and others can interfere in an individual's life. Of course, freedom is not an absolute. We are all constrained by law, by convention, by decisions made by others. These limitations are accepted values that enable us to live happily with others. Thus, the important principle of autonomy is tempered by the rights of others. It is not sovereign. In the case of assisted dying, a person's desire to seek that way out medically will meet the autonomy of his doctor who might say, "On grounds of conscience, I cannot do that." This was essentially the position of the Law Lords in the case of Tony Nicklinson. His desire clashed with the laws of the land and revealed the limitations of autonomy.

Nevertheless, at the centre of the Nicklinson case is a challenging legal asymmetry. A blanket ban on assisted suicide opposes directly a person's right to die if she or he wishes. Yet the courts promote autonomy as a cardinal principle in matters of health. Thus, a rational person has an absolute right to refuse all medical treatment even if the decisions put the patient's life at risk. In the case of Tony Nicklinson the Supreme Court referred several times to the case of Re B (2002) which established that a competent, ventilator-dependent woman had the right to demand that the machine keeping her alive be switched off. Thus, we have the strange situation that the law gives a person the right to demand his or her machine is switched off, but the same law will not allow a dying person to be administered drugs that would enable him or her to die in peace. Lord Neuberger argued in connection with Nicklinson's plea to be allowed to die that, in his opinion, the step of switching off a ventilator, which is permitted, is a more drastic intervention than the setting up of a drug system for a very ill person who requests assisted dying.

As I have mentioned earlier, another huge issue is that of "the sanctity of life", a phrase which has been part of bio-medical and ethical discussion for years. It has been assumed that the concept denotes a strict prohibition on euthanasia and assisted dying. Yet it has to be said that the issue is not as straightforward as many think. It is not, for example, a phrase that occurs in either the Hebrew scriptures or the New Testament. Sanctity, of course, is used many times but in relationship to God himself. When used of human beings holiness is in relation to God: "Be holy, for I am holy." However, in recent years the phrase "sanctity of life" has become little more than a culture war slogan rather than an understandable position based upon serious reflection. I recall that, at a medical/legal conference in Cambridge in 2016, led by Professor Rajesh Munglani, I was challenged to give it some substance. The challenger, a lawyer with a strong history in human rights, asked: "Surely it is time to ditch jargon and focus on meaning? If sanctity of life is only the language of the churches, we must seek more substantial meaning in language we can all agree." I replied that I was sympathetic to his point of view but felt that there was great value in using the language of "sanctity" because it flows from the very best sources of our Western cultural heritage (Jewish, classical, Christian and modern) reflecting the fact that human beings are made in the image of God. The phrase embraces the concepts of infinite value and moral worth. I went on to argue that the concept of the sanctity of life leads to the belief that all human beings of every race, colour, creed, ability or disability, social class or moral goodness are to be reckoned as persons of equal worth and to be treated as such. Indeed, I argued, within such traditions the phrase is not limited to our worth at the end of life but to the whole of life.

Some time after the conference I discovered that Christian theologians and philosophers had rarely used the term until the 1960s. It was with the publication of a book in 1957 by a Welsh lawyer, Glanville Williams that it gained popularity.[17]

So what bearing does this have on issues to do with end of life care and assisted dying? It has direct bearing, of course, on how we treat people, on our understanding of the value of life and its quality. My mind flashes back to the 1998 Lambeth Conference when I met

Matthew, the son of Bishop Mark Dyer and his wife, Elizabeth. Mark was at that time Bishop of Bethlehem in the United States. A former Benedictine monk, Mark left the Roman Catholic Church at the same time as Elizabeth left her convent. They married and adopted three children. The third child came to them just before Christmas. The social services rang and asked them to look after a new-born baby boy who was not expected to survive. The social worker explained, "The little boy has no brain, therefore no sight or hearing. He is unlikely to live more than a few days." The bishop and his wife took the baby and the bishop baptised him Matthew. Perhaps the little boy responded to their love – we shall never know – but he lived, not just a few days, but years. I met him at the Lambeth Conference in 1998. He was a young adult, but still like a baby, in his nappy with a smile on his face, blind, deaf and unable to respond.

I asked Mark to explain: "Did you ever feel you wanted to hand him back to the social services? How could you cope with a child and later a young man who could never grow into a full human being?"

Mark said: "George, he has given us such joy and love. We are richer because of him."

I was humbled by such a wonderful estimate of a human being who might be considered worthless but in the eyes of God has inestimable value.

In the same way, those of us who believe that there is a place for assisted dying for those who request it because of their sufferings also believe in the intrinsic value of every human being.

Beside the issues of autonomy and the sacredness of life is also the concept of "slippery slope". The claim is made that, if assisted dying is permitted, then society will inexorably be led down a slippery slope that will weaken our common resolve to protect the most vulnerable. The introduction of laws which allow people to choose to end their lives will, it is suggested, lead inevitably to abuse of the elderly, sick or weak. This argument is commonly evoked and was there in the Archbishop of Canterbury's assertion in 2016 that to change the law could put vulnerable people under pressure to end their lives so as "not to be a burden". It would leave a "sword of Damocles" over the heads of elderly people.

This is a serious point and warrants examination. There are two parts to it. The first is that permitting a doctor to assist a very ill person to die is open to abuse. The second part is that allowing assisted dying to become part of the law of the land could put pressure on vulnerable elderly people to end their lives, so as "not to be a burden" on their children.

In the case of the first part, it is easier to assert the inevitability of slippery slopes than to prove it. When we consider places where physician-assisted dying (PAS), is allowed and has been practised for years, such as the American state of Oregon, it is impossible to discern any slippery slope. Of course, abuse is always possible when some human beings are determined to find a way around the law. We could take the illustration of driving. There was a time when driving a car was considered so dangerous that a man was required to walk with a red flag in front of a car. Certainly driving was a slippery slope and laws were required to ensure that abuse was punished. People still drive faster than they should, some drive without licences, some drive under the influence of alcohol and some are under-age. But no one has used the slippery slope argument to prove that cars are dangerous and allowing people to drive is a slippery slope with disastrous consequences for the most vulnerable. The reason is that society, through its laws upheld by the police, has protected the public from the negative results of abuse. It is quite unreasonable to withhold from some people a legal right to reasonable activity simply because that right may be abused. Thus, the answer to the first part of the question must be to have well-drafted laws that support the request of those seeking to end their lives while protecting the law from abuse.

The second part – that creating such laws will inevitably put pressure on the vulnerable elderly – is a far more subjective argument but the answer is essentially the same. There will always be some greedy relatives anxious to get their hands on the money of elderly relatives – the answer is strong law as well as social services that protect the vulnerable.

However, we have much more than guesswork to go on. The UK is far from being the only country exploring the issue of assisted dying. Other countries are ahead of us in examining the theme and the experience of those seeking help at the end of their lives: Switzerland, Netherlands, Belgium, Luxembourg, Canada, Spain and the state of Victoria in Australia. In the United States, the states of Oregon, Washington, Vermont, California, Colorado, Washington DC, Hawaii, New Jersey, Maine and Montana all allow assisted dying and/or euthanasia. Yes, indeed, there is variation between some of these authorities and some are unquestionably, in my opinion, better than others. However, in all these places strict controls are in place and legal and medical supervision exercised in all cases. There is no "slippery slope" in any of these places and palliative care is not in decline. Oregon, one of the first places to introduce assisted dying, sets a very high standard of compassionate care alongside an emphasis upon palliative care. The assertion sometimes heard that, where assisted dying exists, palliative care declines is contradicted by the facts. The two are not in opposition.

If Oregon was among the earliest American states to embrace assisted dying, California is among the most recent and one young woman made a sad but important contribution to that state's change of heart. In early 2014 Brittany Maynard, studying psychology for her Master's degree, began to have violent headaches. She sought medical help for what she thought was an ordinary condition only to be told, after thorough and extensive tests, that she had grade 2 astrocytoma, a form of brain cancer. She had a partial craniotomy and a partial resection of her temporal lobe. However, the cancer returned a few months later and was now a grade 4 astrocytoma with a prognosis of six months. Her brain was dying, although her body was healthy and strong and it was possible that her body could live for another sixty years. The excruciating headaches continued but did not put off this young and beautiful woman from finishing her degree and getting married. When it became clear that there was no hope of recovery, she relocated to Oregon as the state of

California did not have a law allowing terminally ill patients to seek a physician's help in dying. On November 1st 2014, at the age of twenty-nine, Brittany ended her life peacefully. Brittany concluded that it was unjust that, although she could afford it, other people less well off could not resettle in another part of the States to get the help she was going to receive. She began a campaign to change the law in California. It was a deep sense of injustice that drove this gifted woman to devote her final months to opening her own life to the public. Her story caught the imagination and the compassion of Californians. The following year a law was passed that allowed the forty million residents of California to have the option of assisted dying should they become terminally ill.

Although the reaction from the general public was sympathetic and supportive, the Roman Catholic Church was outraged and condemned Brittany's action. Monsignor de Paula, head of the Pontifical Academy for Life, reacted by saying, "This woman took her own life thinking she would die with dignity but this is the error. Suicide is not a good thing. It is a bad thing because it is saying 'no' to life and to everything it means."

It is difficult to speak kindly of this statement. Of course, Mgr de Paula was expressing the strong condemnation of his Church towards ending a life under any circumstance. However, she did die with dignity, on her terms, her mother and husband with her. She was not saying "no" to life because there was no quality of life to look forward to as the cancer would have consumed her brain, leaving her with a mindless body. Her husband, also a Catholic, responded to the Vatican's condemnation: "There was no cure. There was no holy site or sacred oil to rub on her forehead to cure her. There was no way to pray away her pain or her tumour."

The following year, in the House of Commons in the United Kingdom a Private Member's Bill won approval to be tested on the floor of the House. Rob Marris led the argument for assisted dying. Sadly the bill was defeated: 118 votes for change with 330 against.

What we can be sure is that the matter is far from over. The medical profession is increasingly following public opinion in favour of a change to the law. In 2019 the Royal College of Physicians dropped its opposition to assisted dying, after surveys of its members found that opposition to a change in the law had fallen under 50 per cent. Similarly, in 2020, surveys of the membership of the BMA (British Medical Association) showed that 40 per cent of respondents were in favour of a change in the law that would allow doctors to offer prescriptions to assist sufferers to have a pain-free death. Only a third of members argued for a continuation of its current policy of opposition. A further 21 per cent were in favour of neutrality.

I look forward to the time when the law of our land will allow those relatively few seriously ill people to end their lives in dignity and on their own terms. I ended my brief address in the House of Lords with the following words:

> As to those who chide me – and they have – by saying that my argument and change of heart are light on theological backing, let me tell them what my theology is all about. It is about accompanying those very sick and dying people to that place where they feel most abandoned, where they are already experiencing their own Calvary or Golgotha, and where they need us to be with them to help them find peace of mind and to help them on that journey. If that is not theology of the best and purest kind, I do not know what is.

9

George Bell, Prophet and Pioneer

Bell was an unlikely campaigner. His was not a striking public presence; his voice was gentle and rather high. He had little feel for the pungent generalisations of rhetoric. More important to him were the intricate facts that lay behind complicated issues. In a world of propaganda and confrontation he perceived that credibility and influence grew above all out of exactitude.

Andrew Chandler

It is impossible to overstate George Bell's contribution to the world and the Church of the first half of the twentieth century. He died when I was in theological college in 1958 but his reputation was already very significant and his legacy was to be felt for many years, especially in the areas of social justice, peace and ecumenical dialogue.

At college I had the fortune of meeting several clergy who knew him, or were ordained by him, and their views were unanimously positive. He stood out. But when asked to explain, few were able to point out exactly in what particular way he stood out. Some spoke of his integrity as a person, others of a "still, quiet determined person" whose ability was without doubt. Following his ordination in 1907 and curacy in Leeds, three remarkable periods of service would cement his reputation as one of the outstanding Anglican leaders of the era. These were his appointments as chaplain to the Archbishop of Canterbury, as Dean of Canterbury Cathedral and as Bishop of Chichester. It is not my intention to outline his glittering contribution to ecumenism and peace in Europe because that has been done in several biographies and none better than that by Andrew Chandler.[18] Dr Chandler quotes Nathan Söderblom, Archbishop of Uppsala, Sweden saying of George Bell as a young man that "nobody is more important to the future of the ecumenical revival than this silent Bell. This Bell never rings for nothing. But when it does ring, its tune is silver-clear." But that was equally true of other areas of Bell's ministry and none more so than his distinguished service as bishop during the war years. He was a giant of faith, a holy man who, as in Geoffrey Chaucer's haunting description of the humble priest in Canterbury Tales,

> ... had no thirst for pomp or ceremony,
> Nor spiced his conscience and morality:
> But Christ's own law and His apostles twelve
> He taught, but first he followed it himself.

That has always been my estimate of him.

But all that was thrown into question when, in 2015, some fifty-five years after Bell's death, a complaint was made to the Archbishop of Canterbury and taken up by the Bishop of Chichester, that George Bell had abused a five-year-old girl. The allegations against George Bell date from the late 40s and early 50s. The anonymous complainant "Carol" originally made her complaint to the former Bishop of Chichester in the late 1990s. At that time, as was so often the case in the diocese of Chichester, the complaint was never followed up. This meant that in 2015, after the Church had failed so spectacularly in a number of celebrated scandals and cases, the diocese of Chichester was now over-compensating for its earlier errors. The accusation was that, in the privacy of the palace (George Bell's home) and also, it is claimed, in the cathedral itself, the bishop met regularly with this child, whose aunt worked in the palace. The current Bishop of Chichester, Dr Martin Warner, and his Core Group, a committee of "advisers", accepted that the accusations were genuine, paid her a large sum of money and apologised for the abuse stating that "the abuse of children is a criminal act". Thus the great George Bell was labelled a paedophile. I was not alone in finding the allegations extremely odd and unconvincing. That a child of five could identify the Bishop of Chichester in that way many years later is in itself an astonishing feat of memory, but she was talking about one of the busiest bishops in the Church of England. Henrietta, the bishop's wife, ran the palace like a well-oiled machine and Adrian Carey, the bishop's chaplain during part of the time, said emphatically that no child was ever seen alone in the parts of the house described by Carol.

Those who raised doubts about Carol's statements were not questioning her sincerity. That she may have been abused by someone was not the issue. There seemed to be a "ring of truth" about her trauma that impressed those who heard her. But her claim that her violator was the bishop needed proof, not hearsay.

Peter Hitchens, journalist at the *Mail on Sunday*, was particularly scathing in his comments about the Church's handling of the accusation. He argued that, although long dead, Bishop George Bell "deserves the simple justice of the presumption of innocence". Charles Moore, another distinguished journalist, wrote in January 2016:

> Bishop Bell died in 1958. When he was thus condemned 57 years later, he had no witnesses in his defence and, indeed, no defence. There are no published records of the process which condemned him. The decision was made by the "core group" of

"safeguarding professionals" and the bishops of the diocese, under the Church of England's National Safeguarding Team. They decided, not on a level of proof that would satisfy a criminal court, but "on the balance of probabilities", that Bell had committed the alleged acts.

It is extraordinary that they ignored the fact that, even when evidence is tested by a civil court on the "balance of probabilities", all sides of the argument are heard. The Core Group erred in not allowing an argument from a defender of George Bell's reputation to be put.

Initially, I was a bystander while this was going on, assuming, as one does, that the Church of England was handling this in a responsible way. But I was prompted to intervene on receiving a letter from George Bell's niece, Mrs Barbara Whitley, who wrote in February 2016 asking for help in responding to the allegations against her uncle whom she knew well. Barbara first got in touch with Peter Hitchens, who relayed her concerns to Dr Andrew Chandler. Prompted by Andrew, Barbara wrote to me expressing her deep distress that no one in authority from the Church had been in touch with her. She was certain from her uncle's known pattern of living that he would never do such awful things to a young girl. I replied to say:

> Your letter has now prompted me to seek ways of reopening this matter. The fact is that the Church of England has effectively delivered a "guilty" verdict without anything resembling a fair and open trial. His reputation is now in tatters and, as you sadly point out, all references to him in the diocese he loved and served have been removed or renamed.

This brought me into the controversy directly. On March 6th 2016 an article appeared in the *Mail on Sunday* under the headline "Carey's fury at Church over abuse case bishop: Ex-Archbishop accuses officials of destroying dead priest's reputation with unproven claims". This article was, in fact, far more measured than that the headline, pointing out Mrs Whitley's sadness that as the only surviving relative she had been overlooked and her testimony not sought.

I then wrote to the Bishop of Bath and Wells, Peter Hancock, who was the lead bishop on issues of safeguarding:

> Of course, if there were clear evidence that George Bell was a child abuser I would not be writing as I am. But there is none. There is rising concern about the way the complaint has been handled on what seems to be the flimsiest of grounds. Bishop George Bell died in 1958 and, in an exemplary life his probity and holiness has never been questioned – until 1995.

I went on to say,

> Though I understand that the Diocese of Chichester may not have reacted properly to the first complaint by Carol, there has been absolutely no justification offered for the way the Church appeared to concede that Bell was "guilty" on the balance of probabilities. There was no attempt to contact Bell's family, nor those of his staff who are still alive, nor to consult his papers or his biographer. A growing number of people now believe that there are strong grounds for the matter to be re-examined, not least for the sake of natural justice. It would be wonderful if you could look into this once more because the good name of the Church is very much at stake – and not least the reputation and legacy of one of the greatest leaders of the nation during the dark days of the war.

I was very disappointed by the answer. The reply from the bishop was a typically bureaucratic response that was, in my view, written in the vain hope of stopping further correspondence. It did not and could not. Even though I was engrossed in the ongoing inquiry into Peter Ball's behaviour at the time, I was very concerned by the way George Bell's reputation was being trashed on the basis of very questionable evidence. A great and noble bishop, long dead, was being treated shamefully by his church.

It was largely as a result of contact with Andrew Chandler concerning Mrs Whitley that I received a note from Frank Field MP inviting me to a meeting to discuss George Bell. Present with Frank were a number of significant people; among them Dr Andrew Chandler, whose recent outstanding biography of George Bell had attracted international praise; Charles Moore, journalist on the *Daily Telegraph* and biographer of Margaret Thatcher; Desmond Browne QC; Alan Pardoe QC; Lord Lexden; Dr Martyn Percy, Dean of Christ Church, Oxford; Dr Anthony Harvey; Dr Keith Clements; Lord Dear; Margery Roberts and myself. Others, including Dr Ruth Hildebrandt Grayson, later joined what became known as "the George Bell Group". The aim of the meeting was to share ideas and to challenge the narrative that George Bell had abused Carol. A convincing case had not been made by the Church that he was guilty, and a wrong had to be righted.

In March 2016 the Bell Group published its own examination of the charges against the bishop and, especially, the accusations by Carol. The Group was not disputing her claim that she was abused by "someone" but poured considerable doubt on the allegation that Bishop George Bell was the aggressor. In particular, the report examined her claim that the bishop would be waiting for her halfway up the stairs and take her into a room and then abuse her. The George Bell Group stated: "There is no staircase on which Carol could have seen the bishop standing. The bishop's kitchen (and for that matter the staircase outside it) was not part of the bishop's domestic residence or where he worked." Canon Adrian Carey, who served as the bishop's chaplain during the early 50s, was emphatic about the bishop's remarkable lifestyle and stated that, from his knowledge of Bishop Bell and the hours which he worked, he found it impossible to imagine how such abuse could have occurred. Since it was his duty to answer the door he knew who was in the house and what activities were taking place. The George Bell Group went on to examine the claim by Carol that she was taken to the palace and put to bed there and that the bishop would use the pretext of reading a bedtime story to molest her. Carol's account of the time spent with her aunt was that she "went for weekends and school holidays, usually for two or three days at a time, sometimes a week". It is inconceivable that if a child was spending such a length of time in the palace, she would not have been seen by the bishop's chaplain or chauffeur. But Mr Monk, the chauffeur, apparently saw nothing untoward and Canon Carey's recollection is quite emphatic: he never saw a child staying in the palace.

However, if such logistical arguments show the hollowness of Carol's claims, Bishop George Bell's extraordinarily busy and dedicated lifestyle is enough to convince all but the wholly prejudiced opponents of Bell. Such evenings as he was at home he spent with his equally dedicated wife, Henrietta, and with the many papers and speeches that he was churning out all the time. All this, and much more, made the Bishop of Chichester's conclusions not only incomprehensible but unspeakably foolish and cruel.

The uproar continued, with the George Bell Group in the midst of the fray. Peter Hitchens mischievously called the group "The Belligerents" and this term stuck. We all saw the cause as worth fighting for, not only to clear the name of George Bell, but also to fight an increasing tendency in Church and society to blacken a person's career on the basis of hearsay and insinuation. The Church has a duty, as we saw it, to protect the innocent from charges of wrongdoing, even if they are dead.

In June 2016 Lord Lexden managed to secure a debate in the House of Lords on the rising number of allegations of historical sexual abuse. He opened a lively debate by going to the heart of the issue, which was the increasing tendency to believe allegations of abuse. He referred to a recent Oxford University report which showed the impact of false accusations against innocent people, leading to unemployment, breakup of relationships and, often, mental suffering. Drawing upon Dr Chandler's recent biography, Lord Lexden went on to say:

> Everything that Dr Chandler has examined reinforced the view that this [George Bell's] was an unblemished life, a model in every respect of what a great Christian leader should be, in private as well as in public affairs. How can a bishop retain his greatness if he is found guilty of a cardinal sin? Here surely is a man who has a special claim to the most careful treatment if posterity should ever have cause to doubt his virtue.

Others voiced different concerns. Lord Dear, a former Chief Constable of the West Midlands Police, made a powerful intervention:

> If she was indeed assaulted it could not have been by Bell. All the geography, the timing and so on speak very clearly. It points to the activities of a cleric who may well have been occupying the nearby theological college, next to the Bishop's Palace.

Perhaps even more radically, Lord Dear expressed deep concern about the nature of the Church's investigation. He said:

> We face a body which, on this occasion, is simply unaccountable and deeply resentful of the most authoritative external criticism. It has misrepresented the arguments of its critics, rather than face up to them squarely, and provided absolutely no information about its processes or identified those responsible for them despite the fact that the reputation of a significant figure has virtually been trashed.

Following Geoffrey Dear's contribution, mine was next and I expressed my dismay that as a result of the hurried judgment against such a distinguished man "a trashing of his memory and magnificent career is now well under way with the renaming of George Bell House and George Bell School and, at the university, the George Bell Hall of Residence." I went on to say:

> The Church of England has admitted that, given the ancient nature of the accusations, the standard of proof was based on the civil standard of probability, not that of criminal standard of proof. However, even the civil standard relies on a person having a defence, someone to bat for them, and we have no evidence that the safeguarding officials of the Church of England – mentioned by the noble Lord, Lord Dear – who oversaw the supposedly painstaking investigation looked at any evidence. For example, I question whether they ever considered his extensive travels or his household arrangements, which might have thrown up some question marks about the nature of the allegations. They did not question a surviving relative or, even more devastatingly, Canon Adrian Carey – no relation – his chaplain for two of the years that the claimed abuse happened.

I concluded:

> I am distressed to make this observation of my own Church, but it seems to me that in this particular instance, its procedures have had the character of a kangaroo court and not a just, compassionate and balanced investigation of the facts.

Baroness Butler-Sloss, a distinguished lawyer and judge, offered as she often does in the House of Lords a penetrating analysis of handling historic abuse cases from the viewpoint of law. She observed that there is a firm commitment in English criminal law to the principle that a person is innocent until proved guilty in a criminal court. In cases where the balance of probabilities is applied, we must recognise the importance of looking carefully at the inherent probability or improbability of the allegations. She then quoted a case in 1996 where Lord Nicholls said, "The more improbable the event, the stronger must be the evidence that it did occur before, on the balance of probability, its occurrence will be established." She then expressed her considerable concern when the balance of probabilities is applied to historic cases of child abuse in which the alleged perpetrator is dead. "I was taught as a young barrister *'audi alteram partem'* – that is, one has to hear both sides." She went on to say that one should give adequate support to people making allegations but "generally – I should perhaps say always – it should resist the temptation to say that the account is convincing and is to be believed. Even on the balance of probabilities, if one side cannot be heard, that in my view is a step too far."

Lord Judge made an important contribution in observing that one has to be immensely careful in assessing the opinion of very young children. "In 1958 Lord Goddard made it absolutely plain that it was ridiculous to suppose that the jury would attach any value to the supposed evidence of a child of five years old."

The Bishop of Chelmsford, Stephen Cottrell, now Archbishop of York, was clearly put into a difficult position responding on behalf of the Church. He began that defence by acknowledging his own indebtedness to the late Bishop George Bell. He then argued:

> It also needs to be said that the core group did have the benefit of legal advice, the views of Sussex Police, evidence about the survivor's connection with the Bishop's Palace at Chichester and medical reports. Church staff also examined the Bell papers held in Lambeth Palace library. The legal advice was that, had the claim been tested by a court, on the balance

of probabilities, Carol would have won her claim. In those circumstances, the proper thing to do was to settle the case rather than putting a survivor through the harrowing process of giving evidence.

This claim, though confidently stated, was thinly argued and dubious by any standard of objective reasoning. Such legal advice that the bishop referred to was later shredded by the independent review, which we will come to.

Stephen Cottrell, however, took exception to my description of the process, saying: "A kangaroo court was a really unhelpful slur in an otherwise serious and helpful debate. There is a review taking place. It is a review of the process which will enable us to learn lessons for future cases." Sadly, the bishop did not pay sufficient attention to what I actually said which was that the process had the "character" of a kangaroo court, which is a wholly different thing. But we were all glad to hear mention of an independent review which was published on December 15th 2017 by Lord Carlile of Berriew QC, a highly respected and internationally known expert in criminal and safeguarding law.

Lord Carlile explained that his terms of reference were not to determine the veracity of the claims against the former Bishop of Chichester but to examine the procedures used by the Church of England's Core Group to reach the conclusions it did. Starting with the original complaint in 1995 Lord Carlile stated that the diocese of Chichester did not serve Carol well when she first wrote to the then Bishop of Chichester, Eric Kemp. Instead of suggesting that she should speak to her local priest, he should have begun a genuine process of inquiry and, perhaps, have met Carol himself. The Church failed her again in 2012 when she wrote to Lambeth Palace and received an "inadequate" reply. While, then, it was entirely proper for the diocese and Church to approach a Core Group to assess the nature of Carol's distress and concerns, Lord Carlile concluded that the Core Group's assumption that the possible damage to a dead man's reputation was considerably less important than the needs of Carol was erroneous: "Whilst understandable and superficially appealing, I have concluded that this approach is wrong."

Then Lord Carlile considered the central argument of the Core Group that on the balance of probabilities Carol's arguments would have succeeded in a court of law. Lord Carlile agreed it was right to rely on the civil burden of proof – proving Carol's allegations on the balance of probabilities rather than the criminal burden of beyond all reasonable doubt. However, the review asserts that if the Core Group had seen the evidence that his review had managed to uncover without great difficulty, the case would not have been thought strong enough even to be tested in court. "No call for evidence went out, no attempts were made to find any other potential victims, no interviews were taken with the surviving staff at the Bishop's Palace, and no contact was made with the bishop's surviving relatives." The review is damning about the inadequacies of the Core Group's investigations.

Lord Carlile noted that, apart from unsubstantiated and anonymous second-hand allegations in a local newspaper which he had been unable to probe properly, no one else had ever come forward, before or after Carol, to accuse Bishop Bell of impropriety. Indeed, the opposite was true. Unlike the Core Group, Lord Carlile took the simple and necessary step of issuing a call for evidence, commonly done is such circumstances. He received convincing evidence of Bishop Bell's propriety towards children.

Although Lord Carlile's brief did not include determining whether Bishop Bell was innocent of the charges, he concluded in his review:

> For Bishop Bell's reputation to be catastrophically affected in the way that occurred was just wrong. I regret that Bishop Bell's reputation, and the need for a rigorous factual analysis of the case against him, were swept up by a tide focused on settling Carol's civil claim and the perceived imperative of public transparency.

The Core Group's key concern was not the justice of the case, for either Carol or Bishop Bell, but the reputation of the Church, Lord Carlile stated. Underlying all discussions was the assumption that Carol must be telling the truth; even by the second meeting of the Group, "any notion of a balanced investigation had been abandoned".

Lord Carlile's report made a series of recommendations about how future safeguarding inquiries should be conducted. The most significant was that alleged abusers must not be named publicly unless an investigating Core Group finds a "proper basis of evidence" for the claims.

Furthermore, Lord Carlile argued, "When a case results in a financial settlement without an admission of liability, as in the Bishop Bell case, there should be a confidentiality clause in the settlement to stop the accused's name ever being published."

The workings of future Core Groups should also be overhauled, Lord Carlile recommended. There must be someone assigned to advocate for the accused or their descendants, and it should be emphasised to those making allegations that the Core Group maintains the concept of innocent until proven guilty. Each Core Group should also include someone with genuine and up-to-date experience of the criminal law and procedure.

At this point the Church should have accepted with grace, dignity and humility Lord Carlile's clinical review but instead fell far short of this duty. The initial responses by Peter Hancock, Lead Bishop on Safeguarding, and Martin Warner, Bishop of Chichester, acknowledged the shortcomings of the Church's response and were effusive in their thanks to Lord Carlile but rejected his central recommendation that alleged abusers should not be named publicly unless an investigating Core Group found a "proper basis of evidence" for the claims. Peter Hancock argued that although he accepted that the Church's processes were deficient, "the Church is committed to transparency. We would look at each case on its merits, but generally would seek to avoid confidentiality clauses."

However, the deepest hurt was then inflicted on the reputation of Bishop George Bell by the Archbishop of Canterbury Justin Welby who in his statement said:

> ... we have to differ from Lord Carlile's point that "whereas in this case the settlement is without admission of liability, the settlement should be with a confidentiality provision". The Church of England is committed to transparency and therefore we would take a different approach. ... The complaint about Bishop Bell does not diminish the importance of his great achievement. We realise that that a significant cloud is left over his name... no human being is entirely good or bad. Bishop Bell was in many ways a hero; he is also accused of great wickedness.

This extraordinary statement aroused great fury among Bell supporters. On reading it I wondered at first if the Archbishop and I had read the same document. Lord Carlile's statement made it clear that the Core Group had been wrong to condemn George Bell and now the Archbishop, no less, was saying that "a significant cloud" rested over his life and career. But there was no cloud, other than in the minds of the very few who were convinced by Carol's testimony. And for the Archbishop to state that that Bishop Bell is "accused of great wickedness" is almost as if he believed it. But there was no proof, and therefore George Bell was entirely innocent of the charges brought by his own diocese against him. An allegation does not lead irrevocably to the conclusion that a cloud remains. If facts do not justify conclusions, the conclusions must be false.

In January 2018 I wrote a personal letter to the Archbishop asking him to clarify what he meant by "a significant cloud is left over his name". I wrote: "I think you have a duty to clarify what you mean and the basis for contending this claim. Lord Carlile's review gives you no authority to do so, and no hint of scandal has been found in George Bell's life."

Even though the Archbishop chose to ignore my letter – not even acknowledging it – the uproar continued with many incensed by the

Archbishop's unwillingness to see the irrationality of his position. A series of letters to the press from distinguished figures then flowed in the weeks after the Archbishop's pronouncement. A letter published in the *Daily Telegraph* on January 18th from a number of historians including Professors Charmian Brinson, Andrew Chandler, John Charmley, Michael J. Hughes, Sir Ian Kershaw, Jeremy Noakes, and Keith Robbins expressed "profound dismay" at the Archbishop's statement after the publication of the Carlile review and called on him to retract it. It argued that the office of Archbishop gave him

> no authority to pronounce on the reputation of Bishop Bell in the manner you have done. We are prepared, in this letter, to claim that authority. We state our position bluntly. There is no credible evidence at all that Bishop Bell was a paedophile ...

> None of us may be considered natural critics of an Archbishop of Canterbury, but we must also draw a firm line. The statement of 15 December 2017 [in response to the publication of the Carlile report] seems to us both irresponsible and dangerous. We therefore urge you, in all sincerity, to repudiate what you have said before more damage is done and thus to restore the esteem in which the high, historic office to which you have been called has been held.

More was to follow. A letter from nine well-known theologians, written largely by Canon Anthony Harvey, expressed shock that the principle of "being innocent until proved guilty" has been rejected by the Church: "Natural Law has been accepted in mainstream church thinking for many centuries; therefore to repudiate it would represent a radical (and deeply unpopular) attack on received doctrine, which again would require very strong moral grounds if it were to be sustained." As for the Archbishop's rejection of anonymity, the theologians stated that it is natural justice again that demands that anonymity is maintained until the evidence is there. The letter argues that, having appointed Lord Carlile, a representative of "temporal justice", to pronounce on the Church's handling of the Bell affair, Archbishop Welby should not have disagreed with one of his key findings – that someone accused of abuse deserves anonymity until the charge is proved – "without advancing strong moral grounds". The letter concludes with a plea to the Archbishop to repudiate his disagreement with a report "conducted with great integrity by a respected lawyer", and asks him to do all in his power to restore the reputation of "one of the most respected, courageous and prophetic church leaders of the twentieth century".

This point was echoed in a letter to the *Daily Telegraph* from Dr Ruth Hildebrandt Grayson, daughter of Dr Franz Hildebrandt, who was a close friend of Bishop Bell. She, more than most of us, knew about the character of George Bell's private life and had no doubt that the accusations were groundless and shamed a truly good man. In a letter to the *Daily Telegraph* dated March 24th 2018 Ruth summed up the grounds for the concern that so many had expressed:

> The continued anger that the case has aroused has nothing to do with Bishop Bell's eminent reputation. It has everything to do with the fact that no one has ever been allowed to present a case in his defence... When will the Archbishop have the grace to admit that the church leaders responsible for handling the George Bell case – including himself – have made the most colossal error of judgement in this instance?

The *Church Times*, in its editorial of January 26th 2018, got it absolutely right:

> It is because innocence is harder to prove than guilt that the UK legal system insists on assuming innocence until guilt has been proved. It is this

assumption that Bishop Bell is being denied, and it is for this reason that Lord Carlile and others have advocated anonymity for those accused of abuse.

The uproar continued with a number of retired judges, including His Honour John Bullimore and His Honour Alan Pardoe QC, adding their authoritative voices to the tumult. "We are grievously disappointed at your failure to show proper regret and to apologise for the great harm and injustice which the Church, through the catalogue of errors identified by Lord Carlile, has caused," they wrote.

In private correspondence long after the events described, Lord Carlile wrote to me:

> At the request of the Church of England, I prepared a report on the process whereby the deceased George Bell, was named, shamed, and his reputation destroyed in relation to allegations of sexual impropriety and assault towards a child of a Bishop's Palace staff member in the 1940s. My review was evidence-based, after a public call for evidence which produced important responses. I concluded that the investigation fell well below proper legal standards, and that the finding made against Bishop Bell should not have been reached, applying the civil standard of proof. I found too that the public acceptance of his guilt on the basis of unproved allegations was wholly unjustifiable. I made several recommendations for a more legal complaint process for the future. My recommendations have gone largely ignored or misunderstood. This is a great disappointment to me.

But more surprises were to come. Later in the January 2018 more allegations that Bishop George Bell was indeed a sex offender were made by a woman who was referred to pseudonymously as "Alison".

The Church of England's national safeguarding team announced on January 31st that it had received "fresh information concerning Bishop George Bell". The statement gave no further details on the grounds of confidentiality, but then continued: "Sussex Police have been informed and we will work collaboratively with them." Lord Carlile could not contain his astonishment at the release of news about a new allegation. He remarked in an interview with the *Daily Telegraph*:

> I am not privy to the information that is referred to in the Church's press release. But I think it was unwise, unnecessary and foolish to issue a press release in relation to something that remains to be investigated, and which was not part of the material placed before me over the period of more than a year in which I carried out my review. During that period the review was well known, and it was open to anybody to place information before me.

However, this time the national Church did react in a responsible manner by appointing a former police Detective Superintendent Ray Galloway to carry out an investigation and the Bishop of Chichester appointed Timothy Briden QC to conduct a review. Mr Briden's report did not take long to publish its conclusions as it quickly became clear that Alison was eager to support Carol's account to such a degree that she repeated verbatim actual statements of Carol's. Chancellor Briden concluded in his report that the new allegations were "inconsistent", "inaccurate", "unconvincing", or, in some instances, amounted to "mere rumour". Her testimony was dismissed as baseless and all her allegations unfounded.

The question remains, as Lord Carlile hinted, at the timing of the second allegation. The allegations concerning Bishop Bell had been known for some time – why did Alison intervene at such a late stage? Was it a clear attempt to silence the critics when the Church and the Archbishop were so squarely cornered, to buy time and to create a public belief that Bell was, after all, a predator? We shall never know but it may well have had the opposite effect and have reinforced George Bell's reputation as a noble and holy man.

As we entered 2019 there was a general feeling within the George Bell Group and the wider supporters of Bishop George Bell that all arguments had been spent and it was now futile to expect the Archbishop of Canterbury and the Bishop of Chichester to withdraw their statements. In an important article in the *Church Times* (February 1st 2019) Dr Chandler expressed his own sadness at the Archbishop's judgment by concluding:

> After three-and-a-quarter years, it is surely time to make a decision. We might join the Archbishop of Canterbury, Dr Warner, and their safeguarding managers as they shiver in self-justification under their own significant cloud. Or we choose a different company and walk honestly as in the daylight in the company of the historical George Bell himself, an innocent man who is now more than ever vindicated by responsible, authoritative opinion.

Indeed, Andrew was correct. Authoritative opinion, a free and critical press and an informed public opinion, both within and without the Church, vindicated Bell. There were many who raced to the defence of the bishop. Within the diocese of Chichester the pen of Richard Symonds was particularly active and, in time, he was to acquire a national reputation for his spirited and sacrificial defence of George Bell. Although profoundly deaf, this did not stop Richard from a campaign for the former bishop that went beyond protesting letters and emails. Richard used his own money to set up conferences in London where supporters and opponents could meet and discuss in a spirit of openness and charity.

Later in 2019 the George Bell Group disbanded. The Group had gone as far as it could and it was felt that, although we had not achieved our goal of clearing the good and proud name of Bishop

George Bell, sensible people in the future would realise that there was no basis for the shameful charge that he was a paedophile.

Personally, I was left very puzzled by the failure of the Archbishop of Canterbury and the Bishop of Chichester to recognise the errors of their logic against the overwhelming support for the long dead George Bell. Leadership, surely, includes the capacity to recognise when one has made an error of judgment. Sadly, it seems that the only reputations wrecked and ruined were those whose rigidity of opinion had dumbfounded everyone. No cloud remains to stain one of the giants of twentieth century Christianity, George Bell.

10

A Family Nightmare

The past is a foreign country; they do things differently there.

L.P. Hartley

The famous first line of L.P. Hartley's *The Go-Between* summarises the problems inherent in the tension between what happened in the past and our experiences now.

This is certainly true in the area of the enormous and rapid changes in human sexuality over the last fifty years or so. I was ordained in 1962 when the majority of marriages took place in the Church of England, according to the Book of Common Prayer. If there were different attitudes towards sexual behaviour they were not talked about openly. But change was in the air. As Britain emerged from the austerity of the war years, and began to enjoy rising living standards, so attitudes towards sexual mores began to relax. The failure of Mary Whitehouse to combat the publication of *Lady Chatterley's Lover* in 1960, together with exciting trends in music and theatre – to say nothing of advances in contraception – led to a greater tolerance and openness and ultimately to what became known as the "sexual revolution" of the 1960s.

At the same time young people pressed for autonomy which resulted in the age of majority being reduced from twenty-one to eighteen in 1970.

It was astonishing to discover that in 1275 the age of consent was twelve. It was only in 1875 that it was raised to thirteen in 1875 and then, in 1885, raised again to sixteen, where it has since remained. Homosexual reform came, following the the recommendation of the Wolfenden Report, and homosexual acts were decriminalised in 1967, the age of consent being set at twenty-one. This age would be lowered in 2000 to sixteen to be in line other forms of sexual activity between consenting adults.

Thus, while much attention amongst law-makers was given to adult sexual law reform, adults, far less attention was being given to those under-age, who might be victims of abuse. Sexual abuse was considered to be very rare and, if it occurred at all, went on only where living conditions were poor or amongst people of low ability. However, the twentieth century was a time of gradual discernment and change. The Children's Act 1908 established juvenile courts and, extraordinary to notice, the Punishment of Incest Act gave the state jurisdiction in a matter which had previously been handled by clerical intervention. Further improvements to laws protecting children were introduced in 1932, 1948, 1968 and 1974 until 1989 when the Children Act gave every child the right to protection from abuse. There was general ignorance concerning sexual predators and the distress and harm caused by those who preyed on the most vulnerable. Needless to say, these laws protected only children and had little or nothing to say about "vulnerable adults".

Ignorance and naivety were shared by most of us in the mainstream churches. For myself, my priority and commitments were about honouring my marriage and ordination vows. I regarded deviation from either as sacrilege of the highest kind. And the behaviour I expected of myself, I expected of other clergy as well. However, I was not so naïve to believe that priests never deviated from their ideals – but such activities rarely occurred in my circle of ministry and experience. I was, therefore, very unprepared when the greatest church scandal in my time of office came before me.

In this chapter and the next I shall narrate the painful events to do with Bishop Peter Ball that have taken up so much public attention in recent years. I ask the reader's patience as I go into detail and reflect on the story. There have been two national inquiries which have judged me sternly but I have had only limited opportunities to put my point of view.

I had just returned from a two-week visit to Sri Lanka in my second year as Archbishop, when, on December 11th 1992, Bishop John Yates, my Chief of Staff at Lambeth Palace, told me that the twin brothers, Michael and Peter Ball, wanted to see me urgently. Michael was the Bishop of Truro and Peter the Bishop of Gloucester. Michael I knew very well as a godly and excellent church leader because he had been Bishop of Jarrow and, therefore, my bishop when I was Vicar of St Nicholas' Durham. But I knew of Peter only by reputation. He was renowned, particularly in Anglo-Catholic circles, as a very popular preacher whose work among young men was greatly admired. His scheme, known as "Give a Year to God", had led a number of young men to offer for ordination – indeed, several had passed through Trinity College, Bristol, where I had been Principal.

In that very difficult meeting, arranged for Tuesday 15th December, I could scarcely believe what I was hearing – that a bishop was being accused of the sexual abuse of a young man. Peter vehemently denied it and Michael backed him completely. It was nonsense and should be strongly rejected, they argued. I then met with Peter Ball privately and he continued to dismiss the allegations, pointing to personal jealousies in the Order of which he was part as an explanation for a "conspiracy" against him. Dr Frank Robson, Provincial Registrar and legal adviser, had rushed from Oxford to be with me and arrived late for the meeting. It is horrifying that no note exists today of that meeting, a deeply unsatisfactory outcome.

Events moved very quickly from that moment. There was strong public support for Peter from within the diocese of Gloucester and nationwide. I, too, could not believe the accusations against him and publicly gave him support. On a day-to-day basis, John Yates was in charge of dealing with any developments including much of the correspondence because over the next few months I was to undertake trips abroad to Sri Lanka and South Africa, as well as my usual visits to Canterbury and throughout the Church of England. We decided to ask Bishop Ronald Gordon, former Bishop of Portsmouth, and Dr Frank Robson to investigate the charges. Regrettably, this was a mistake. All three were older men than I was, and likely to have even less awareness of child abuse in society. I should have entrusted that task to people with greater experience of abuse but was misled by a desire to keep this confidential and in-house.

In the meantime, Peter Ball had become progressively ill. He was under the care of a Truro psychiatrist. Reluctantly he accepted the police caution against him and resigned from active ministry, retiring to Truro to be with his brother. My attitude to Peter Ball changed accordingly. My earlier support gave way to a sad acknowledgement that he had betrayed Christ but it did not seem to me that there was anything else I could do. The criminal side of the matter had been handled by the police and I had been told in no uncertain terms that it was none of my business. When I made enquiries of the police seeking information of the exact details of the allegations which had led to his "caution" I was told it was a police matter.

Looking back to that period I realise I made two fundamental mistakes. I trusted Peter Ball too much and failed to put him on the Lambeth Caution List. This list was intended to bar priests from returning to ministry without counselling, repentance and renewal. The decision not to place him on the list was made after consultation with Frank Robson, my lawyer, and John Yates, my Chief of Staff. Although it was my decision, we reasoned together that Ball was now retired, very ill and would never work as a priest again. What we failed to see at the time was that, as Ball's health improved, he would seek any means to return to a limited ministry to redeem himself.

Throughout this entire period John Yates was alongside to

guide and share. As I was often away or abroad, John's role was to be the resident bishop, representing me vis-a-vis other bishops and the government. I did not know at the time that John Yates, who had preceded Peter Ball as Bishop of Gloucester, had written, in the controversial 1979 "Gloucester Report" on homosexual relationships, the following observation:

> It is clear that there is a class of child molester, who is typically attracted by young children (often of either sex) whom he wishes to fondle or whom he invites to touch or inspect his genitals. Such behaviour, more pathetic than immediately dangerous, is understandably greatly shocking to the parents of the child, and in some cases the child himself will be frightened and disturbed, though there may be no long-term ill effects.

I do not cite this in criticism of Bishop John Yates who was a valued colleague. Yet in spite of being a reformer and a progressive, he was also a man of his time. Many decades later I also found out that only weeks before Peter Ball was arrested on suspicion of indecent assault on the young novice Neil Todd, Bishop Yates was visited by Mr and Mrs Moss, gardeners to the Bishop of Gloucester. This couple, who counted Bishop Yates as a friend, having worked in the palace gardens when he was Bishop of Gloucester, had befriended Neil Todd and taken him on holiday with them to flee Bishop Ball's increasingly violent threats towards the young man. It seemed that John was in full possession of at least some evidence about Ball which he did not share with me or any of his colleagues at Lambeth Palace.

The role of the Gloucester police in this matter troubled me as well. I tried to find out what the actual charges were against Ball that had led to him accepting a caution (thereby admitting his guilt of a minor offence) and which resulted in his resignation. I was told that the decision was made and that was that. I gleaned that Ball engaged in sexual acts which fell short of penetrative sex. Whatever they were, they were shameful for anyone to indulge in, let alone a priest and bishop. I was left with other questions sparked by some of the letters received at Lambeth Palace. How many young people? One young man was certainly under the legal age of consent of twenty-one at that time and other young men were involved. Lambeth Palace had received letters from a number of people and I and my colleagues sought to reassure them that we were handling the matter responsibly. I was certainly not covering up this embarrassment – it was after all being investigated by the police.

However, one particular aspect of the Peter Ball scandal would haunt me later: letters which had been received at Lambeth Palace and were undoubtedly mishandled. I had asked for an investigation by Bishop Ronald Gordon to ensure that the letters were properly followed up. He then in turn took legal advice from the Provincial Registrar. I was shocked to learn in 2017, during an interview with Dame Moira Gibb who was conducting a review into the Church's handling of the Peter Ball case, that the Gloucester police had visited Lambeth Palace and had asked see correspondence of relevance.

When I expressed the depth of my surprise on hearing this, Dame Moira undertook to check. She subsequently wrote to my solicitors on December 14th 2016, to the effect that, although she had not had formal confirmation from Gloucester police, she had heard evidence from the officer who had led the investigation at the time, Deputy Chief Inspector Murdock, who had visited Lambeth Palace on December 22nd 1992, but was given only one letter. She continued, "There was no suggestion of course that the Archbishop knew about this meeting." She later confirmed that Mr Murdock said that he had met with Bishop John Yates.

However, in her report, she did not provide this clarification that she was making "no suggestion" that I had any knowledge of the meeting. In fact, I was in my study when police apparently visited and, according to dates on the letters, I was replying to two of the letter writers. One was a mother who had raised concerns about

Peter Ball's behaviour towards her son. I wrote to her stating that if she had any concerns she should write directly to Gloucester police. On the same day, I also wrote personally by hand to one of the victims, who had been a student of mine when I was Principal of Trinity College, Bristol. My letter shows that I was extremely shocked and moved by his letter. Sadly, however, he did not seem at the time to be describing a criminal act, although now, years later, I would automatically have understood that I was seeing the patterns of abuse and behaviour which are now widely recognised. At that time I would have greatly benefitted from the sort of training which is such an important aspect of clerical development today.

To this day I remain astonished at this chain of events. There is no record of the meeting between John Yates and the police, although I now know it took place. I wish that John Yates were still alive to give his account. According to DCI Murdock, who made the visit, John Yates only handed over the least incriminating letter of seven which had been received at Lambeth Palace. This gave rise to the appearance that we had deliberately denied evidence to the police. Looking back at those letters, it is now clear that police interviewed the large majority of those mentioned in the letters at the time, which contradicts Murdock's later speculation that, had he seen the letters, the police would have treated this matter more seriously than by merely cautioning Peter Ball. In fact, contrary to this, Gloucester police and the Crown Prosecution Service have both now said in evidence to the Independent Inquiry into Child Sexual Abuse (IICSA) that they ought to have dealt with Ball differently at the time on the basis of the copious amount of evidence that they already had from a large number of witnesses.

Additionally, the letter writers all described different experiences of Peter Ball. Some of them explicitly stated that their letters were intended to be confidential, and one of the letter writers revealed that he had already contacted the police. Another of the letter writers recounted as a positive experience with Peter Ball something that would have been disturbing and uncomfortable for other people. Others gave no detail of their encounters with Ball. Indeed, Peter

Ball at the time was attempting to explain aspects of his behaviour, particularly the prevalence of nudity and cold showers with young men, in terms of "Franciscan spirituality". This was arrant and deceptive nonsense, and an important reason why he had to resign as a bishop.

Sadly, this conclusion that Lambeth Palace had failed to hand over letters goes some way to explaining why Dame Moira shockingly concluded in her statement to the press when her review was published that, "Cover-up and collusion fall on a spectrum that includes carelessness and partiality", in a context which clearly indicated that this was her judgment on my involvement. This was immediately seized upon by the media and by Archbishop Welby, who quickly assented to the idea that my carelessness and partiality amounted to cover-up and collusion and requested (in effect) my resignation as an Honorary Assistant Bishop.

Another matter of which I have been accused is knowing about the activities of Peter Ball's defence team in employing a private investigator, Brian Tyler, to try to discredit the accounts of Neil Todd and other accusers. Having set out to exonerate Ball, Tyler interviewed a number of witnesses and concluded that there was considerable evidence that Ball had subjected young men and boys to sexual abuse and violence. The Bishop of Chichester, Eric Kemp, provided some funding to Tyler and even allowed him to surreptitiously record an interview with police. John Yates also held a meeting with Tyler. In his written reports, Tyler comes across as a "Walter Mitty" type character with name-dropping pretensions and exaggerating his own credentials, abilities and connections. In one of his letters he states that his report is written for Eric Kemp and the Archbishop of Canterbury. The incriminating report, however, to my certain knowledge never came across my desk and, in fact, was eventually found more than two decades later in a filing cabinet in the Diocese of Chichester. It proved to be the key document which enabled police to open up their investigation into Bishop Peter Ball, resulting at last in a successful prosecution in 2015.

However, returning to the middle of 1994, I and my colleagues at

Lambeth did believe that the Peter Ball affair was over. The man had retired in disgrace, his ministry as Bishop of Gloucester was now over and we could all move on. Regrettably, the following months and years would tell a different story.

First, Ball himself staged a full recovery and in spite of claiming to be deeply ashamed, continued simultaneously to insist on his innocence. He then pressed me for permission to take services, particularly to resume his ministry preaching in public schools. In the vast majority of cases the invitations came from people who admired Ball's ministry and some felt I was being very unkind to this disgraced bishop by continuing to refuse him permission.

However, from the perspective of years later we are now able to view more objectively the activities of people like Peter Ball and, later, Jimmy Savile. Both men operated in organisations where their degree of success and popularity gave them an aura of untouchability. And, in both cases, the evil they did was the sordid flip-side of the skills that made them successful. Much later, I could see that Ball had been playing me with his tears, his cries of "I am totally innocent!" and protestations that he was the victim of people who wanted to silence his effectiveness as a bishop. Sadly, he had much support. Lord Lloyd, an eminent Lord of Appeal and one of the most astute judges of the 1990s, badgered me constantly to allow Ball back into ministry as a bishop. Heads of public schools, members of the Houses of Commons and Lords, countless members of the dioceses of Gloucester and Chichester, bishops and others, believed Peter Ball to be totally innocent and, in the view of some, the victim of a vicious campaign.

Gradually he was allowed back into limited forms of ministry, under supervision, but was always a constant thorn in the flesh wanting more ministry and even started making noises about launching a legal challenge to his police caution.

Then the shocking revelations in 2012 of Jimmy Savile at the BBC led to increasing attention to historic cases of abuse in other organisations. Rightly, the spotlight returned to the Ball case, as new evidence was unearthed.

So it was that, years after my retirement, scrutiny of the Ball case took place, kick-started by considerable alarm about a "cluster of cases" by prolific clerical abusers in the diocese of Chichester where they had apparently operated in a culture of impunity for years.

Safeguarding specialists painstakingly reviewed files held by the Church of England and discovered a "long lost" file in the palace in Chichester which included Brian Tyler's report for Peter Ball's defence that contained considerable evidence of abuse of young men and boys. This was reported to Sussex police who reviewed this alongside earlier evidence by Gloucester police and came to the conclusion that Peter Ball had been let off far too lightly with the caution in 1993 and decided to pursue a new investigation. This led to a trial in 2015 and a prison sentence of thirty-two months.

These events resulted in my years of retirement being increasingly oriented towards dealing with the aftermath of Peter Ball's abuses. As Archbishop of Canterbury the buck stopped with me when it came to the church's mishandling of this. But this had to be placed alongside the failures of the police and prosecuting authorities.

A lessons-learned review was commissioned by the Archbishop of Canterbury led by an eminent former social worker, Dame Moira Gibb. And later, the government IICSA took upon itself to examine the scandal of Peter Ball as a separate case study in its strand on the Church of England.

Eileen and I were sitting at breakfast at the Sloane Club in London on October 19th 2016, prior to a short holiday, when Eileen received a call from our daughter-in-law Penny. The news was devastating. My elder son, Mark, had been arrested that morning. A woman had made a complaint that when she was a young girl Mark had violently sexually abused her. She claimed that Mark had abused her over a period of years, starting some thirty-eight years earlier when she was seven and Mark only twelve. Penny phoned us in distress after the police had conducted an early morning raid on their vicarage in Harrogate. Police were searching the house and Mark had been taken to Durham to be interviewed. Andrew, our other son, was able to find a very able defence solicitor in Harrogate to give Mark swift advice and representation. It was immediately obvious that our holiday had to be cancelled and we must go to Harrogate to be with Mark and Penny and their family. We were at their home when Mark returned, looking distraught, yet dignified. He reported that the woman in question had been a childhood friend of Lizzie, our youngest daughter. The accusation was that Mark had violently abused her when she stayed at our vicarage with Lizzie. She claimed that she often had sleep-overs at the vicarage.

The story sounded highly suspicious to us. When the children were not at school the house was busy and filled with noise and laughter. Rachel, Mark, Andrew and Lizzie got on very well and no room was ever closed. Furthermore, Eileen insisted that sleep-overs were extremely unusual events; on rare occasions a friend of one of the children would stay if there was an emergency at home. But this girl's home was only a matter of minutes up the road and she never stayed at the vicarage. The description the woman gave of the vicarage was inaccurate in many ways. And the picture of our young and innocent teenage son was unrecognisable from the monster she had invented. Mark was shattered by this cruel ordeal, but worse was to come. The following day a social worker appeared to establish guidelines for Mark to follow in the family home. Thankfully none of his three children were young, otherwise he would likely have been ordered to leave his home. But he was told that he must not remain alone in the same room with his children, Danny and Grace, both under 18. He was also informed by the diocese that he was suspended from ministry and must keep away from his church and, indeed, all other Anglican churches in the diocese.

Eileen herself was interviewed the following day by two policewomen and I was asked to leave the room. Although we had been assured of strict confidentiality in a matter of days the press had the story and pictures started to appear in the *Sun* and *Daily Mail*. Indeed a photographer with a long-lens camped outside the house for twenty-four hours until he got the picture he was after – of Eileen and myself.

We all felt helpless as the process continued. A process that gave anonymity to the complainant and none to the person accused felt invasive and unjust.

Each member of our family was then interviewed with the exception of myself. The two policewomen travelled to Canterbury, Devon and Somerset to interview Mark's siblings – Rachel, Andrew and Lizzie. They answered truthfully and credibly that the claims of abuse were untrue and unsupported by any evidence. That Mark as a young teenager did such gross things to a seven-year-old was palpable nonsense. They knew their brother, and we knew our son.

This presented the diocese of Leeds with an opportunity to show that it cared in its support for one of its clergy but, sadly, it failed in a number of significant ways. I would have expected the diocesan bishop to meet at once with Mark to outline the pastoral care they would offer him. There was no such meeting. The Bishop of Ripon, the suffragan bishop, was appointed to look after Mark. Although a very kind man, his support was limited because he lacked the authority of the diocesan bishop. Meetings with the Bishop of Ripon were intermittent and rarely informative.

Mark's own church, Kairos, was tremendously caring and shocked but Mark had been instructed to keep away from his church. They in turn were led to believe they should not contact him. Within days, therefore, all support and contact with his clergy friends and church dropped away. Mark was abandoned and it hurt us all deeply. The days and months passed. We were with Mark at Christmas and stood with him as he attended the midnight service at Beckwithshaw Church led by his friend Guy. We were delighted that, despite the lack of diocese support, his friends had rallied around him.

There were financial challenges on the way. We felt that we should get a good lawyer to support Mark and guide him through this intolerable period. Eileen and I gladly raised the necessary funds for their legal costs. The diocese contributed only towards some personal costs that Mark and Penny had to meet. It grieved us that the diocese seemed to care so little. On March 15th, on my way to the library at Lambeth Palace, I bumped into the diocesan bishop, Nick Baines. I felt I had to say directly that I was shocked by the lack of care offered to Mark. The bishop was offended and said that two bishops had been appointed to care for Mark. That I said was not the case. The Bishop of Ripon who was about to retire was replaced by another bishop. The Bishop of Leeds and I parted unhappily. He later somewhat redeemed himself by taking the decision to reinstate Mark rather than let the National Safeguarding Team make Mark wait for no good reason.

If our family felt that Mark and his family had been treated uncaringly by the diocese, we were delighted when on April 5th the police contacted Mark to say that they were taking no further action. The allegation laid by the woman was dismissed. The legal advice had been that it was very rare for the police to drop a case before taking it to the Crown Prosecution Service but clearly there was so little substance to the allegations the police felt confident about this decision.

There was no fanfare from the diocese to greet Mark's complete exoneration. The diocesan safeguarding process then began to consider risk assessment, rather than simply lifting the suspension. This made it seem that the diocese believed there was still a case to be answered. At this point Mark, who had been extremely cooperative and patient, dug his heels in and refused to cooperate with risk assessment on the ground that this false accusation dated back over thirty years, the police had found no evidence to corroborate the woman's claims and there was no reason to question his ability to continue his ministry. Disappointingly the diocese failed to review and reflect on the effect this whole affair had upon a clergy person, his family and the local church – instead they chose an internal review, no doubt focused on reputation management.

However, the government is at fault as well. As the law stands, innocent people are routinely accused and lives ruined because police officers have decided that allegations of child sex abuse should always be believed. Lord Lexden, an eminent historian much devoted to social matters whom I have quoted above in connection with the George Bell Group, has raised several questions in the House of Lords calling for anonymity for those accused of unproven crimes but, to date, has had no satisfactory reply. It is an injustice which demands resolution.

Within a few months Mark, having had his name cleared, moved to another diocese and to fresh ministry. His experience did not give any of us confidence in the pastoral care of the Church of England.

11

Accused

All men make mistakes, but a good man yields when he knows his course is wrong, and repairs the evil. The only crime is pride.

Sophocles, *Antigone*

It was not long after Mark returned to ministry, bruised, saddened but still determined to serve Christ fully, that my ministry received its most serious rebuff. On June 20th 2017 the long wait ended when I received Dame Moira Gibb's full report with the damning title *Abuse of Faith*. She focused all of her attention on me, and very little on the other figures in the Church of England at the time, who had mostly passed away. Although I knew that the buck stopped with me as Archbishop, the Church of England was not a command and control structure. Dioceses themselves had considerable autonomy. As I have related above, the report seemed to single out me personally with regard to claims that I had failed to hand over letters to the police.

Next day a brief email arrived from the Archbishop of Canterbury with an attachment about the report. His letter asked me to talk with the Bishop of Oxford and told me in no uncertain terms to relinquish my role as Assistant Bishop in the diocese of Oxford. I was astonished by the lack of pastoral care. He had not bothered to request a meeting and tell me face-to-face; there was no attempt to phone me – only an emailed letter. I did phone Steven Croft as requested and found him caring and sympathetic. But he was as insistent as Justin Welby that I should stand down. We agreed to meet the following Saturday morning with Eileen present, along with my son Mark.

The following day, June 22nd, the Archbishop held a press conference about the Gibb Report and his tone was condemnatory. The report, he said, made harrowing reading. "The Church colluded and concealed rather than seeking to help those who were brave enough to come forward. This is inexcusable and shocking behaviour," he declared. The accusations of collusion and concealment were particularly hurtful and damaging because I knew them to be untrue, not least in the light of the extensive police investigation which took place in 1992 and 1993.

Eileen and I, together with Mark, met with Steven Croft and his chaplain on Saturday, 24th June. Bishop Croft attempted to be pastoral but it was becoming clear that, in asking me to stand down as an Assistant Bishop, he was forcing me to relinquish my entire priestly ministry and thus was effectively "laicising" me.

This was a shocking step and I felt as though I was being sentenced without trial. I pointed out to the bishop that his letter to me contained this sentence: "If you determine not to take this course of action [to stand down] then, as you understand, I will need to consider whether I will at that point need to revoke your licence for a season." Strangely, he did not consider this a threat.

Almost immediately the consequences of the action emerged. I was forbidden to preach the following Sunday at Wargrave Parish Church; I was unable to speak at a friend's memorial service in the Bristol diocese; I was told I could not participate in a charity event in the Oxford diocese and, immediately, the Bishop in

Europe informed me that an invitation to address clergy in Zurich was withdrawn. More punishment was to come as charities and organisations we had supported over the years cut their ties. It was especially hurtful being asked to stand down as President of Lee Abbey, Patron of the Salmon Centre and Patron of Work Aid. In the case of Lee Abbey, a Christian conference centre in north Devon which we had supported for many years, I was perfunctorily dismissed.

The feeling of abandonment was real. I was deeply concerned for Eileen and the effect on her. One's loved ones are often the ones most deeply affected by the actions of their partners and this was particularly so in her case. She had always been a rock in our relationship, never complaining about the workload that came with my ministry. She now felt punished and rejected. In her despair she decided that she could not receive communion at church until my ministry was restored. Our local parish church, St George's gave us a great deal of support at a difficult time. The following day, June 25th and our fifty-seventh wedding anniversary, the minister in church, the Rev Terry Winrow, spoke movingly of the support and affection for us both. The fellowship and support of the congregation was the principal reason for us feeling that we still belonged in the Church of England.

This brought to the surface a major question: where did we belong spiritually? For some time, particularly because of what had happened to Mark, we had begun to question whether we could remain in the Church of our births. We felt as though we were being cast into outer darkness. Could we remain in a body so condemnatory and uncomprehending? But where could we go? We did not feel at home in non-liturgical Churches; the beauty of worship was deeply important to us. Ever since I studied at Rome in the 70s I had been drawn to the Roman Catholic Church, and felt that we could settle there, even though there were aspects of theology that could be difficult. Additionally, we felt uneasy about joining a Church which rejected the ordination of women. Both of us found the question of "where did we now belong?" shocking and distressing. We felt that we had to overcome the initial bitterness and learn the deep lessons of the cross, that my, and our, calling was to follow and serve Christ – not the fallible body that we felt was rejecting us.

Of course, we had plenty of support. Besides our local church, there were hundreds of friends who rallied around, and through their letters and emails encouraged and cheered us on. One of those was the Archbishop of York, Dr John Sentamu. I had known John and Margaret a very long time and, indeed, had consecrated him Bishop of Stepney. Although there was little John could do publicly, I think he was very perturbed by the way his colleague at Lambeth was handling it. John later wrote, "I still find it hard to understand why anyone put it to you that you had to relinquish your licence as Assistant Bishop. There were no legal processes initiated against you by anyone."

I was particularly encouraged by an article in the *Daily Telegraph* by Charles Moore, an outstanding writer and journalist. Entitled "Our great institutions must not be pulled down in the hunt for sex abusers", Charles questioned the Archbishop's use of words like "colluded and concealed". He remarked:

> Colluded and concealed are strong words. They describe not bad judgment but iniquity. Even Dame Moira, though she uses them, inserts qualifications. Archbishop Welby does not. Does he truly think that Lord Carey committed iniquity?

I was very grateful for those words of understanding but I felt that I had to build relations with the Archbishop of Canterbury. Having sat in his seat, I knew from experience how difficult that role is and believed that a personal meeting between us was necessary. I expressed my bewilderment that I was being judged by the standards of today rather than by the standards of the early 1990s. I wrote:

> It is the historic perspective that is largely absent from the Gibb Report. The report pays lip service to

the fact that things were very different back then but, as I read it, I am condemned in the light of modern processes, cultural attitudes and guidelines. Dame Moira even suggested in a BBC news interview that I had failed to follow procedures. I did not have the benefit of any procedures in those pre-Savile days. The failure – on her part – to take this factor seriously is a huge oversight. I acknowledge my mistakes. You will have seen my apology. As the Archbishop at the time I was in charge, and must take responsibility. But the allegations you yourself made were of "collusion" and "cover up" which in my opinion go beyond the judgment of the report and may even feed these very distressing and damaging assertions that I should be prosecuted.

In that letter I requested a meeting so that we could discuss this in a Christian way. The reply which I received six days later refused a meeting on the grounds that if anyone made a complaint against me under the Clergy Disciplinary Measure he, as Archbishop, would be compromised if he had previously met me, because he as Archbishop would have to chair any such disciplinary matter. I was astonished by this reasoning and could not understand why he was not willing as a priest – as well as an Archbishop – to meet me pastorally. In fact, I believed he was badly advised because it was extremely questionable that any of my actions in the 1990s could come under the Clergy Discipline Measure which only came into effect in 2003 after I had left office.

However, one startling point he made in the same letter was that, as a young curate, he had been "well aware of the need for what today we would call safeguarding", by implication suggesting that I should have been too. The answer to that is simple and clear; no safeguarding processes were in place at the time. There was no training, no policies and the term was certainly not in common use.

The months passed. I was in limbo as far as Church ministry

was concerned and the next thing on the horizon was the long wait for the IICSA chaired by Professor Alexis Jay, to report. In the intervening months, a prominent lawyer, Jonathan Caplan QC, asked to see me in his chambers. We met and he looked over the letters received from the Archbishop and the Bishop of Oxford and at once agreed with John Sentamu's viewpoint that no one had the legal authority to deprive me of ministry. In his opinion, it was a matter of natural justice. He wrote at once to Steven Croft pointing this out and insisting that steps should be taken to give me Permission To Officiate. After an exchange of correspondence and a meeting, permission was reluctantly given. Six months later I was able to officiate and Eileen felt that was the right time for her to start to receive communion again.

This, however, was not the end of the matter, for the IICSA was already sending me reams of questions to form the first of four witness statements that I was to submit over the next year. The Church Commissioners were gracious enough to pay for a barrister, Mr Charles Bourne, in addition to continuing the efficient services of Susan Kelly, a solicitor. And preparations for IICSA took over my life.

On Tuesday, July 24th 2018, I appeared before IICSA. There was a great deal of public as well as press interest in the day's activities and I was quite apprehensive. The whole day was given over to my role in the Peter Ball case and the interrogating barrister was Ms Fiona Scolding. I could not but smile at her surname which I was sure she would live up to. However, she was very fair as well as very sharp and knowledgeable. Six hours of interrogation was extremely tough and I attempted to answer as factually and fully as I was able. I acknowledged that I was too partial to Ball and taken in by his protestations of innocence. I also emphasised that I felt great regret in hardly paying any attention to the victims of Ball and their anger, distress and suffering. I said that I should have listened more to them. My mistake was to assume that support and pastoral care were being supplied to them in the respective dioceses where they lived. But that was not sufficient. . The issue of the letters came up. I emphasised again that no one at Lambeth had deliberately hidden letters from the police. I had no knowledge of visits by DCI Murdock and had never met him. Bishop John Yates, sadly departed, had left no notes of such visits and I was quite sure that John was the kind of man and bishop who would never deliberately hide anything from the police.

The inquiry also focused on the role of Prince Charles and his friendship with Peter Ball. The Prince was not present but had replied fully to searching questions from Professor Jay and her colleagues. Prince Charles acknowledged his long friendship with Ball but stated that he had no knowledge of Ball's crimes. Like myself, Prince Charles was taken in by the man's guile.

Charles Bourne, my barrister, appeared before the inquiry on the last afternoon of that week. I could not have had a better Counsel than he. He made it clear that I admitted my mistakes and regretted greatly ignoring the victims of Ball's deeds and he dealt very clearly with the claims made by the Archbishop of "collusion" and "cover up". As for the claim that the Gloucester police had access to the letters, he showed that there was nothing in the letters that the police were unaware of. Indeed the police had interviewed, back in 1992 and 1993, most of those referred to in the letters received at Lambeth Palace.

I had to wait several months before the inquiry published its report on May 9th 2019. It made very painful reading. I and my staff at Lambeth Palace were criticised for protecting the Church's reputation, as well as that of Peter Ball. I received considerable criticism for providing "personal and vocal support to Peter Ball". This I could not deny and looking back, even now, feel the shame of being so blind. Even though others were criticised, such as the Gloucestershire Constabulary, the criticisms directed at me were severe as well as personal. However, I was not able to agree with the inquiry that I and my staff deliberately misled the police concerning letters we received about Ball's conduct. The inquiry concluded that of seven letters received at the time, Lambeth Palace passed only the least incriminating one to the police. This suggests that the remaining six letters were "withheld". That was not the case. As Charles Bourne argued at the inquiry, there was nothing in the six letters that the Gloucester police did not know. One thing that was sadly missing from the IICSA was, in fact, the historical dimension. There was no recognition of the huge cultural difference between 1993 and 2019. From the viewpoint of 2019 it seems lamentable that conscientious and dedicated Christian leaders could be so blind towards the sufferings of vulnerable young adults, so pastorally uncaring, and so taken in by a selfish bishop who was so used to getting his own way. Yet that is the reality when we look back from a situation where safeguarding structures are present and where Church and society are far more aware of the evil of pedophiles and men like Peter Ball, Jimmy Savile and others.

One notable fact was that the inquiry did not follow the lead of the Archbishop in accusing me of "collusion and concealment" and it was a better and more comprehensive report than that of Dame Moira Gibb. I felt a sense of relief when the IICSA report was published. I was in my eighties and had studied tens of thousands of documents, and letters from some thirty years before and then had answered hundreds of questions in detail to submit four witness statements at the statutory request of the inquiry. I had also been cross-examined exhaustively for an entire day. At last it is all over, I thought. How wrong I was.

An aspect of office of any kind is that one has to put up with criticism and abuse (as well as approval and praise) at every turn. It is par for the course and if it does not stiffen your resolve and give you an extra tough skin, you are unlikely to last long. So I was not surprised when in early 2020, some six months after the IICSA hearing, the BBC broadcast a two-part programme on Peter Ball. I had been asked by the BBC to participate but after taking advice, I declined. I had already participated with IICSA in an inquiry which was more exhaustive and comprehensive than the BBC could hope to do. I realised also that the programme was focused on giving survivors the opportunity to give their viewpoints. I did not expect my opinions to be considered fairly and objectively alongside their palpably difficult experiences. I was glad that the point of view of the survivors was heard sympathetically. In meetings with the Church of England's National Safeguarding Team, I had offered to meet with survivors, but this was never pursued by the church authorities.

I received many emails and letters as a result of the programme. There were a small number which I can only describe as "hate mail"; others were critical, accusing me of protecting the reputation of the Church above everything else. I answered every one of the letters that I saw, acknowledging where I and the Church had failed but also pointing out where the correspondents were wrong in their judgments. Some of them even changed their minds about me. On two occasions when I received emails which appeared to disclose abuse, I passed these onto the Church's safeguarding advisers to ensure these were properly followed up.

Then, to my great surprise, I found myself drawn into a completely different scandal. John Smyth QC came into national prominence in the 1970s when he represented the morality campaigner, Mary Whitehouse, against the *Gay News* and won the case for her. Outside his successful legal career, Smyth chaired the Iwerne Trust, a charity that supervised summer camps for public school boys. Overtly a conservative, evangelical Christian, Smyth was also a sado-masochist who used his links with Iwerne camps to beat boys for his own pleasure. I knew nothing of him and, as someone with a humble state school education, I had no knowledge or connection with the world of public schools.

Towards the end of May 2020 I was informed that the Church of England was going to examine its links with Iwerne camps and I was asked to contribute to it. I agreed, though nonplussed because to my knowledge I had had no dealings with Smyth. However, I learned to my great surprise that Smyth had taken a short sabbatical at Trinity College, Bristol in the summer of 1983 when I was in my first year as Principal.

On June 4th 2020, I had a Zoom meeting with Mr Keith Makin. Mr Makin, a former senior social worker, was employed by the Church to mount this investigation which took place, in the midst of the first Covid-19 lockdown of 2020, via Zoom. I told him I had no memory of Smyth and the only staff member who remembered him was my colleague, Dr Peter Williams. Mr Makin asked if I had any knowledge of two letters that featured my name. I replied that I was unaware of such letters. There was nothing in that Zoom interview that bothered me or suggested that I was connected in any form with John Smyth.

It was therefore a huge shock on June 17th to get an emailed letter from the Bishop of Oxford depriving me, yet again, of my Permission to Officiate as a minister within the diocese of Oxford. So, for the second time I was banned from ministry and considered a safeguarding threat to others.

To my rescue came two remarkable QCs who had become good friends in recent years. Jonathan Caplan QC had already represented me earlier following the Ball accusations, and Lord Carlile QC had carried out the Bishop Bell Inquiry and remained troubled by the approach of the Church to such cases. Both were appalled at the way my ministry was taken away and both considered the charges questionable in the extreme.

It took two weeks of emails passing between us and Mr Anthony Clarke, the Provincial Safeguarding Officer, to make any sense of what I was being accused of. An ex-policeman, Mr Clarke was friendly and polite but somewhat slow in replying to our questions. Eventually we got to the bottom of the charges. In the course of the Makin investigation into John Smyth two letters, both from the Rev David MacInnes to the Rev David Fletcher mentioned my name. I did not know either of them well. They were prominent evangelicals, greatly respected for their preaching ministries. The first letter, dated June 1983, merely referred to a helpful letter that I had written. The second, dated a year later, was from a puzzled David MacInnes wanting to trace two copies of "Mark's memo" which may have described Smyth's crimes. He mentions that David Jackman, minister of Above Bar Church, Southampton, had a copy and so had "George Carey". But then the letter goes on to suggest that the memo could easily be in his own "excellent filing system".

On the basis of this meagre information a Core Group was formed and came to the judgment that I had seen "Mark's memo". Thus I was a safeguarding risk. Whilst this investigation was going on I was instructed to do further safeguarding training supervised by two social workers, which the National Safeguarding Team had promised to arrange nearly two years previously, after the Peter Ball hearing. The training included writing four pieces of reflection over 500 words each. The aim was to check whether I was capable of recognising abuse.

This protracted examination made me consider very closely my memory: could it be that I actually did see this awful memo and was therefore guilty? I gave thought to this because "'the heart is deceitful and dreadfully wicked" as the book of Jeremiah declares. But these thoughts did not last long. I was and am confident that I did not see anything of this magnitude and know my own reactions to awful deeds that I would never stand by and allow evil people to get away with such crimes. And let me be clear to those who say that I had seen such explicit evidence of the crimes of Peter Ball so I am not to be trusted. In fact, as I have tried to spell out, the evidence I saw about Peter Ball was extremely unclear, and at the same time I was hearing Ball's protestations of innocence. Indeed it took the police themselves three investigations before they managed to bring Ball to justice. In the case of John Smyth, the evidence was explicit of beatings of young boys and Smyth had admitted to this terrible behaviour. As I had been the father of teenage children at the time, it was inconceivable that I would have calmly read something so awful and then gone home to my own children and failed to make the connections. As Andrew Graystone, a leading campaigner for the victims of Smyth, wrote to me about the memo: "It is so shocking that I can assure you that if you had been presented with Mark Ruston's 1982 report you would remember it for the rest of your life." Whatever the Core Group may conclude, based upon letters written by others, my conscience is clear; I had nothing to do with Smyth and there was no reason whatsoever for anyone passing to me such a dreadful document.

Nevertheless, in a process which took more than seven months, a Core Group led by the Bishop at Lambeth, Tim Thornton, who works directly for the Archbishop of Canterbury, concluded on the basis of these two extremely unspecific letters that I had seen evidence of Smyth's crimes. They also concluded that I posed no safeguarding risk some thirty-five years after the events had passed, and I would no doubt pass such information now to the relevant authorities. I welcomed the latter conclusion, but to this day am still stung by the former conclusion. This is because they entirely ignored the evidence of Canon Peter Williams, a colleague at Trinity College, who insisted that any communication about a student would have been handled by the staff together. Indeed, no one remembered Smyth at all, and it is clear that his aim at the time was to go to a provincial college where he would be unknown, having experienced such a recent scandal. Peter Williams provided detailed evidence of the way correspondence was dealt with at the college including his own memory of Smyth, evidence that contradicted the Core Group's contention that I had known.

Looking back now at the whole stream of events, four conclusions are worth considering by future leaders of the Church.

First, the Ball scandal did not get the attention it warranted by myself or my staff. At the time at Lambeth Palace we were juggling the storm of controversy that had arisen from General Synod's vote to ordain women as priests and there was also the matter of a Royal divorce on the cards. No one gave the scandal their full focus and held the strands together. The most I did was to appoint a retired bishop to follow up the letters which Lambeth Palace received. This was not sufficient at the time, and it was not until the end of the 1990s that we appointed the first "safeguarding" adviser. To some extent, I feel I did not treat this matter as a priority, as I would now. This was quite wrong because it concerned people who had been let down by a bishop of the Church and was therefore of infinite importance. I regret that neglect.

Second, and of equal scale but with disturbing theological implications, was that throughout my time as Archbishop I had considered that any crime, any sin, was redeemable and every sinner could be brought back into Christian ministry. I had approached Ball in the same way. Although clearly he could never return to work as bishop or priest in a full-time capacity, my belief was that a sexual offender was the same as any other offender, capable of returning to ministry after a period of time. Reflection now on this matter leads me to conclude, sadly, that it is unwise for any offender of this kind to return to ministry in the Church. This is of momentous significance for Christian ministry, because this conclusion assumes that sexual sins are worse than all others and on a par with the "sin against the Holy Spirit". If a sin is forgivable does this also convey the right for an offender to be offered a fresh ministry even if he has committed a sexual offence? This matter needs further consideration by the Church.

Third, in spite of genuine concerns that the Church should reflect the best practices in safeguarding for the sake of its members, it is undeniably the case that safeguarding in the Church of England has become an industry in its own right, often unjust in its treatment of ministers and presumption of guilt. The House of Bishops has largely abdicated its disciplinary powers in favour of safeguarding staff who may, or may not, share the same beliefs as the Church. I have been told that, at the time of writing, there are more than forty bishops who are being investigated for alleged failure to report abuse. This has led to a culture of insecurity and fear.

Fourth, this entire experience has led me to reflect deeply upon the nature of the Church and the role of senior staff within it. We occupy these great offices for only a very limited time. It is our duty to offer faithful ministries within them, doing everything in the name of Christ and his church. That we fail is, of course, a reflection of fallibility and sin, but few of us do so with intention to harm the body we serve faithfully. Even when its servants fail, the Church has a duty to respect what they have done and not cut them loose. Archbishops and bishops have pastoral as well as disciplinary responsibilities to their clergy and predecessors. The duty of care reaches back as well as forward. This is in danger of being forgotten.

Surely the time has arrived for a truly independent and professional disciplinary procedure, comparable to those applicable to doctors, lawyers and teachers?

12

Hearing the Music of the Future

A man said to the universe:
"Sir, I exist!"
"However," replied the universe,
"The fact has not created in me
A sense of obligation."

Stephen Crane, *War Is Kind and Other Poems*

Meaning has always been a central theme in my life. It came to the surface, I suppose, during those bleak war years when everyone was so insecure. My best friend, Harold, did not turn up to school after a particularly bad night of bombing because he and his family had been killed. At the age of nine I did not have the full capacity to frame the existential questions about the meaning of life but the senselessness of it, sadness and horror, were distinctly present. For me, it was rather like being given a jigsaw puzzle without a clue or pattern how to start making sense of it.

My work, when I was in Iraq serving my National Service as an airman, was that of a wireless operator. I was one of six young men who were trained to help the aircraft land at the air force base in Shaibah, near Basra. It meant going to a hut filled with radio equipment three miles out of the camp. It was a lonely job for eight hours at a time. When on duty one never saw a human being unless it was a passing Bedouin family looking after their sheep. I especially enjoyed a night shift. It was pitch black and the stars above shone so brilliantly. Indeed, they seemed to be so close that one felt you could reach up and gather them. It was during my eighteen months there that I came across Blaise Pascal's lapidary comment:

> When I consider the short duration of my life, swallowed up in an eternity before and after, the little space I fill engulfed in the infinite immensity of spaces whereof I know nothing, and which know nothing of me, I am terrified. The eternal silence of these infinite spaces frightens me.

I never felt terrified; indeed, rather the reverse, because it was during one of my periods on duty that I felt a strong calling to follow Christ and be ordained. But I could certainly empathise with Pascal's feeling about the infinite immensity of creation. We know much more now about the cosmos than Pascal did in the seventeenth century. The European Space Agency informs us that there are about a hundred thousand million stars in our own galaxy, the Milky Way, and about a hundred thousand million galaxies in the universe.[19] Our minds cannot take that in. There are various ways we may react to that. There are those who do not seem to be bothered by that fact. I am very sympathetic towards those whose lives are so hard that existential questions of this kind are a luxury they cannot afford. Such an attitude is, possibly, a judgment on the kind of education they have received that a sense of curiosity in their lives has not been awakened.

There is a larger group of people who find meaning in simply living it. They say, "Such existential questions cannot be answered. Life is to be enjoyed. That's all there is to it." I will be harder on this group because life is more than a spectator sport. For Abraham

Loeb, Chair of the Astronomy Department at Harvard University, meaning is found in recognising the intelligibility of life and allowing it to change our lives. And this is why the Jewish-Christian world-view unrepentantly sees all our wisdom and knowledge as emanating from God, creator of all things. We all take it for granted that the universe operates according to laws that are in force everywhere. My coffee neglected will always get cold, and my kettle will always whistle when it reaches boiling point. These laws make science possible because there is an underlying intelligibility that allows human beings to change our environment and shape it. Indeed, we are the only species on earth that has the ability to do so. John Habgood, an eminent scientist, argued that modern scientific knowledge is indebted to philosophical assumptions derived from the Christian faith and particularly its theology of One God:

> Only belief in an orderly creation made to be what it is
> by the sovereign will of God (and hence not deducible
> from anything prior to that) was able to provide for
> those first scientists the philosophic framework they
> needed.[20]

I am aware, however, that there are those who are so overcome by the infinite character of the universe that the claims of the Christian faith seem pathetic and impossibly incomprehensible. If there is a creator of this vast universe what understanding may we give to a personal creator who knows and loves us? It seems simply childish to call "him" a "Father".

But why is it childish? If this amazing, incomprehensible universe came into being through the action of a creator, his character as a caring father – remember these are analogies – is completely understandable and natural.

Making sense of life is basic to what it is to be human, and judging by the way we all seek to find meaning it seems that a religious sense is hardwired into our lives. In Saul Bellow's book *Herzog* the central character states: "People are dying – it is no metaphor – for lack of something real to carry home when the day is done. See how willingly they accept the wildest nonsense."[21] Immanuel Kant put it more profoundly in the conclusion of his *Critique of Pure Reason*: "What can I know? What ought I to do? What may I hope for?"[22] Here are the seeds of faith that have fed the lives of the majority of human beings down the centuries – the conviction that behind the wonder of the universe, there is a Mind that cares. Indeed, the majority of people believe this today and find hope and meaning in a faith that demands some form of ritual by way of response.

Nevertheless, Western life and culture have changed and we have all changed along with them. It is not too sweeping to say that in a sense we are all agnostics now – even the most believing of us – because the habit of disbelieving has become the default system in us all. This is not necessarily a bad thing; to question is central to education and it should apply to all aspects of knowledge. The result is that for so many the world has changed out of all recognition. For some, wherever they look the old signposts are either no longer there or, even if they bother to look for them, have no meaning. The Church has also been affected deeply by the changes in our society and by the hollowing out of faith and belief. We end up struggling to make sense of life in a world where everything is in flux and little appears to be true. The result is timidity and fear. We believe – but not too strongly. Survival has replaced mission and a Church that I recall as being confident and strong is now weak and apologetic.

Some would conclude, sadly, that there is no way back. I recall visiting Norway some years ago and entering a beautiful and well-kept Lutheran church with a group of British tourists. Our guide said flatly on answering a question from one of the visitors about the role of the church in Norway, "The church has no future. It is finished." Some of the expressions on the faces of the tourists around me revealed shock at these words and, later in the day, a few sought me out to get my reaction. At the time, however, I took our guide aside and questioned him on those words. "Are you aware," I asked, "of the formidable work of the Norwegian Church in terms of humanitarian care in the world – hardly an example of a frail and dying faith?" I told him of my experience of working with the Norwegian church in Africa and the wider Lutheran family. Although a nominal Lutheran he had no knowledge of that. Indeed, his disturbing comments flowed more from ignorance.

Some would say of the Church of England that it is dying out and soon will be dead. I totally disagree although the fact of decline stares us in the face. Wherever we look in the Western world the churches have been emptying, and there have been claims that the census of March 2021 will show that Christians in the UK could number 50 per cent or less. This should cause us no alarm. The fundamental causes for the deep chasm between the Western world and Christianity lie beyond the scope of this book, and there are plenty of writings that explore the alienation. But we have no excuse for timidity, for our failure to put mission first and for making maintenance our priority.

The mission of God (not the mission of the Church) is far from over. Great work is still going on in many parts of the Church – and it is this work I have seen over and over again.

But we need to be honest and confront facts as they are. There are strong reasons for unbelief and I have faced them in my experience as a human being and a minister. In three areas of life believers are challenged to think deeply about faith; these are science, personal experience and culture.

Human ingenuity in science is the exciting exploration of the remarkable world around us resulting in huge benefits to the human species. We take for granted what can only be called the "miracle" of scientific achievement. We have taken the raw ingredients of nature and, through the brilliance of human intelligence, have produced vaccines to improve the health of billions. I am writing this during the Covid-19 pandemic. Within nine months of this terrible virus starting to plague the lives of millions, scientists produced vaccines that give hope to us all. It is a staggering testimony to the power and reach of scientific achievement. Little wonder, then, that science is seen as a new "god" who delivers what its worshippers need. But we should remind ourselves that science is only as good as the aims it is set to achieve. It was scientific ability that made it possible for the atomic bombs to be released over Hiroshima and Nagasaki in 1945, killing around 200,000 people, mostly civilians. The morality of that act is still questioned today, some seventy-five years later. Similarly, it was brilliant German science that lay behind the power of Nazi rockets that destroyed much of London. Science is a neutral tool. It may be used for bad as well as good ends. So, we must be careful about treating science and belief in God as opposites. There are many Christians working in different fields of science who perceive their task as a vocation.

But personal experience has also a role to play in our understanding of faith. It may be because of personal tragedy or the sheer randomness of life's chances that some are led to conclude there cannot be a personal God. Many a priest has faced a distraught relative who has asked him, "Where is your God in this mindless pain and death?" No words can reassure people in such predicaments. And we have all been there. Who has not felt the tug of unbelief through events of life that raise major questions about God's presence with us? Among the many great people I have met in my life one man stands out – Elie Wiesel, Nobel Prize winner and Auschwitz survivor. We met at a World Economic Forum meeting where he gave an address. Earlier I had an opportunity to meet him over drinks. I found a shy, frail man, with a firm handshake and friendly smile. He was asked to speak about his belief in God and he referred to a passage in his book, *Night*.[23] He recounted the time in Auschwitz when the SS hanged two Jewish men and a youth. As the young man hung there, an angry voice shouted: "Where is God now?" Wiesel found himself silently saying: "Where is he? He is here. He is hanging there on the gallows." Wiesel meant by this that circumstances change us. For him the presence of such evil and the indifference of the Nazis to the sufferings of others could only mean one thing – the presence, not the absence, of God.

Culture also plays a crucial role in faith formation. If our background has been one of attending a church with a strong community life, we are likely to have a positive view of religion and its role in civic and personal life. Oddly, in my case this was not a factor. My family's connection with organised religion was very distant and church-going was not our habit. My own discovery of the importance of faith was more by intellectual exploration than by nurture in a community. However, habit is an important factor. If a person has had no exposure to organised faith, no encouragement to explore the mystery of faith, or to ask the most basic "whys" of life, then he or she is likely to drift through life without need of a compass.

There are, of course, many reasons why individuals believe or do not believe, and thoughtful people should be encouraged to explore the philosophy of what it is to be a human being. At his trial in 399 BC Socrates uttered the famous line: "The unexamined life is not worth living." Whilst I for one would reject the unconscious bias towards elitism reflected in this dictum – because many people struggle to make sense of life as they live hand-to-mouth, exhausted and poor – Socrates was actually encouraging Athenians to think deeply and less superficially. The same challenge must be levelled at all of us today. There can be no good news of faith if it does not engage or connect with the world in which we live.

So where do we find these points of contact?

Primarily it has to start with us. I have already described my own journey of faith starting from the war years after which I read deeply and reflected on the challenging difference between the horrendous evil of war and the beauty of the Christian gospel. My journey is rooted in encounter: a meeting with the historic Jesus, a journey proven to be true as a result of many years of experience. I remember my fellow Archbishop John Habgood, Archbishop of York, to whom I have already referred, returning from a three-day retreat to do a BBC debate with other scientists on the "existence of God". John, laughing, told me that his fellow scientists were nonplussed when he began his contribution by saying, "How can I talk about believing in God's existence when I have just spent three days in his company?" Habgood took exception to the idea of "Infallibility" in all its forms – and that included science. Awe, wonder and curiosity were central to his science as to his faith in God. Doubt, for him as for me, was a necessary ingredient in life as in faith, to drive us forward, to know more, in every discipline of knowledge.

But there is more to faith than that. The idea that believers simply hook up to an idea which has no content is simply untrue. The content is experience; the experience of knowing that God is with us. The Welsh poet R.S. Thomas spoke hauntingly of God as "that great absence in our lives" but his work as a cleric and his entire oeuvre as a poet never suggests that faith is merely a rumour. Christian experience of walking with God, trusting him in the bad as well as the good times, is a revelation of his presence with us. Hence John Habgood's laughter and words earlier, "I have just spent three days in his company." In the words of 2 Timothy 1:12: "I know whom I have believed and am persuaded that he is able to guard that which I have committed to him against that day." And that claim to know God and his salvation is a constant theme in scripture from the time of the apostles to Paul of Tarsus, St Augustine and through the centuries. Pope John Paul II stated in *Donum et Mysterium*, "The minister of the Word must possess and pass on that knowledge of God which is not a mere deposit of doctrinal truths but a personal and living experience of the Mystery." If a believer cannot say something similar he has no right to speak in the name of Christ and anything he says without experience will always sound hollow.

That is not all we should say, however. There can be no true renewal of faith in local congregations unless clergy remain rooted in the faith and excited by its mission. The evidence is there to be seen in its impact in people's lives as well as in the gospel's influence in its two thousand-year history. Thus, I have to say, from my experience of teaching in three theological colleges and being Principal of one, that the future of faith resides in intelligent clergy, shaped by learning and the discipline of prayer and worship. Yes, I admit to having a love-hate relationship with theological colleges, as they exist at present. Naturally, it is important to lay a good foundation of academic learning in the traditional disciplines of scripture, history, languages and philosophy, and we have many dedicated and able teachers in our colleges. But little good will come of neglecting the missionary context in which we live. Students need to be inspired by teachers and bishops who have known success in building up congregations and leading others to baptism and faith. I am still waiting to see this become a reality.

Equally from my experience, retaining the freshness of faith, combined with an eagerness to learn new things and impart them to others, is essential to growing congregations. No priest, no minister can lead another person to know of the incomparable wonder of the living Christ unless that thirst remains within them throughout life. I recall with much admiration Jack Marden in the diocese of Bath and Wells. An older clergyman than I when I was Bishop, Jack was the much-loved minister of Locking. He had an impressive men's fellowship and was a popular preacher. But the secret of his successful ministry was his undisguised commitment to his congregation. He was a true shepherd to them – visiting them, caring for them, phoning them if he was unable to visit. He was indefatigable.

Thankfully, priests and ministers like Jack are not rare; there are plenty of them about, but they need encouragement and support. Effective ministers need able laypeople to draw out the fire and steel in their makeup.

But there is another thing, almost of equal importance, and that is embracing a love of the world, its cultures and learning. The theological word is "inculturation" which, as the word suggests, implies taking the culture of the world around into our understanding and living. Of course, that has to be qualified. There is much in the world that cannot be tolerated or loved. We immediately think of human selfishness which leads to wars, murders and hatred of others. From a Christian perspective the blanket word is 'sin'. This negative side has been well explored down the centuries. Less well explored has been the link between the positive features of the world in which we are set and the role of the Church, which has often been expressed in the rejection of the world. But there is nothing wrong in retaining and developing a love for the amazing creation all around us and the incredible story of humankind's learning from which culture and art have flowed. One of the most fascinating features of the growth of the early Church seems to have been the quality of Christian leadership. St Paul is an impressive example: a man of learning and erudition who could hold his own with philosophers in Athens as well as with the cultured but ill-taught new Christians of the Corinthian church. As one moves out of the New Testament period into the second century we find learned and confident Christians – Justin Martyr, Hippolytus of Rome, Tertullian, Irenaeus and others – arguing with the sceptics of their day. Being at home in our world, embracing what is good and beautiful, yet rejecting what is harmful, unites our modern, needy world with theirs.

A highly contested view is that one of the weaknesses of Protestantism – a family of faiths to which Anglicanism belongs – is its neglect of aesthetic theology by which is meant art and beauty. A proponent of this view was the Jesuit scholar Hans Urs von Balthasar who in his quite astonishingly erudite seven-volume work *The Glory of the Lord* criticises Protestants for such emphasis upon an interior gospel that the beauty of faith and the glory of the works of God are either ignored or side-lined. Indeed, he quotes one writer who claims: "Whoever loves beauty will freeze in the barns of the Reformation and go over to Rome."[24] (Vol 1.69). Admittedly, von Balthasar praises the attempts of Karl Barth and Martin Luther to extol the beauty of the cross, but criticises them both for their subjectivity. He is fair and yet also unfair in his criticism. When we study the history of art we can see the powerful Catholic imagination as it played upon the mystery of Christianity's beginnings through the medieval artists. Who can doubt that Michelangelo's profound gifts were not influenced by his personal faith? The unfairness of von Balthasar's conclusion is, influenced by his dislike of European Protestantism, that he ignored the fact that the English Reformation was truly a *via media* for it retained beauty, art, prose and poetry as true tools of conveying the glory of God.

Sir Roger Scruton saw a unity in philosophy which must hold objective facts together within the culture from which it emerges. Aesthetics, in all its forms, points to the heart of learning. Although not a philosopher of religion in any conventional way, Scruton found in an aesthetic awareness of the world around us intimations of the transcendent. What he points to in his many writings is something that is central to Anglicanism. We have upheld this in our care for our beautiful buildings and even more so in the scaffolding of our faith — the Book of Common Prayer, the King James Bible and the beauty of liturgy. This is our rich heritage and it is central to the story and future of Christianity in our land and world. Bishop George Bell, the subject of an earlier chapter, saw an unbreakable link between art and faith. "Music or painting or drama, sculpture or architecture," he wrote, "there is an instinctive sympathy between all these and the worship of God."

Who can doubt that this rich cultural heritage is central to the communication of faith today? When I was vicar of St. Nicholas' Durham, I used to play squash against one of the teachers in the Classic Department in the university. Apart from our eagerness to keep fit we had little in common. Michael was an agnostic and kept reminding me of it – perhaps he did not want me to see him as a potential convert. But when we did talk together after a game, we found common ground in appreciation of great works like Dante's *Divine Comedy* and of the way that the Fathers of the Church never rejected the Greek and Roman classics of the past. Perhaps if we had carried on playing squash that appreciation of the beauty of literature might have progressed into a deepening of faith on my friend's part. Perhaps.

Reflecting on the amazing way that art, literature, poetry and music have interpreted Christianity and made it part of our cultural heritage is also part of the startling way that Christianity has shaped our world. It would be the most ironic and saddest element of all if, defeated and disillusioned by our apparent failure to conquer our "cultured despisers", we were to forget that Christianity has had startling success in making much of the world what it is. In his book *Inventing the Individual*, the political philosopher Larry Siedentop quite convincingly shows the role that the Christian faith, and in particular Christian morality, has played in shaping us all.[25] It was, he argues, from the hinterland of Christian thought that the concept of the dignity of the individual arose. A particular feature of Christianity's great influence upon social thinking, Siedentop shows, was the changed position of women. Instead of viewing women as chattels, as was mostly the case in the Roman and pagan world, Christianity saw women as precious children of God, with equal standing to men before him. From this spiritual understanding of women, the idea of their supposed inferiority began to retreat. Siedentop's book is an impressive and convincing argument for the way that Christian beliefs and moral practices have shaped the Western mind and world, and so much so that we have taken it for granted.

While Siedentop has argued that Christianity has shaped the individual, Tom Holland in his book, *Dominion: The Making of the Western Mind*, ambitiously presents the case for Christianity having shaped the whole of Western society.[26] Tom Holland's scholarly habitat is the classical world of ancient Greece and Rome and he shows in the opening chapters of his book the nightmare of the world into which the fragile faith of Christ was born. It is impossible for us to imagine the brutality of societies upheld by state violence of unimaginable terror, the limitless appetite for spectacles of human degradation, and the pitiless infrastructure of slavery underpinning society itself. In that world the tale of the Christian faith was so absurd that scarcely anyone would have given it any hope of success. Holland traces the unlikely story of a supposed "criminal", crucified on a cross, emerging as leader of a Jewish sect that came within the space of a few years to dominate the world, without violence and on the basis of a creed in which love was central. Whereas Siedentop's argument focused on the way the Christian faith shaped the Western world's concept of the individual, human rights and the worth of every human being, Holland's book takes an even more daring stand: the West is the West because of Christianity. Secular, humanist, agnostic or however we identify ourselves, we are shaped by the Christian faith and wholly in its debt. Our deepest values at the heart of Western thought – our belief in the equal dignity and worth of each person, endorsement of universal human rights and the values and worth of democracy – all have their roots in the soil of the Christian faith.

At first sight, Holland's argument seems extraordinary and doomed to fail because of the scope of its claim. Holland is unapologetic, however, and argues persuasively that the Christian revolution continues to shape the world. Towards the end of his book Holland mentions his aunt Deborah, to whom the book is dedicated. As his godmother, she followed his life and career with her encouragement and unswerving faith. Even when he rejected her faith as he grew up, he found it impossible to reject her influence on his life, and in this he found a parable for the influence of Christianity upon the world.

> To be a Christian is to believe that God became man, and suffered a death as terrible as any mortal has suffered. That is why the cross, that ancient implement of torture, remains what it has always been: the fitting symbol of the Christian revolution.[27]

And then, in the final few paragraphs, Holland explains why he chose the word "Dominion" as the title for his book. It is in the audacity of the cross, in the defeated and broken body of a Jew from Nazareth that the sheer strangeness of Christianity is to be found. "God chose the weak things of the world to shame the strong." (1 Corinthians 1:27) So it was in the inversion of power that true dominion is found and it was through the channel of faith of Jesus of Nazareth that shaped and made the Western mind.

Although Holland's book presents a powerful argument for the continuing relevance of the Christian message – the opposite is unthinkable – it is not uncontroversial, and the arguments will continue to run for years to come. Nevertheless, *Dominion* argues convincingly that Christianity is the most influential and enduring legacy of the ancient world that continues to transform our world.

Significant writings of the weight and character of Siedentop and Holland's books (together with Peter Brown's impressive *Through The Eye of a Needle*, which shows the contribution of the Christian faith to philanthropy and care for the very poor[28]) illustrate the substantial vigour of Christian thought and action. How can we, and why should we, lose hope when this has been our legacy to the world? This story is far from being over. This living faith is quite capable of reinventing itself again and again.

However, even if the faith essentially remains the same – the life-giving encounter with the Lord of life – the body in which it comes will change, as it has done, through the years. The other day, I saw a slug in our tiny patio garden; it was bloated and unable to move. Not an attractive picture but it made me think of the Church and a report that appeared in February 2021 entitled *Money, People and Buildings*. The report was understandably concerned about the cost of our wonderful buildings and the implications of maintaining them for posterity. But I found myself questioning the central principle of the document. Anything that starts with money is certainly wrong. If our concerns are mainly about holding on to what we have, we shall never find the inspiration to rejuvenate faith and achieve growth. Furthermore, cutting clergy numbers to balance the books will never halt decline.

What will?

I recall Robert Runcie, when he was Archbishop of Canterbury, enunciating an important truth: "The centre of the Church," he said, "lies on its circumference." It is easy for those who work in our many centres of leadership – Church House Westminster, cathedrals, diocesan headquarters – to assume that in these places the important decisions take place and here is where the future is shaped. This is not true. The centre exists to serve the circumference, the place where true growth happens. Just as the roots of a great oak exist to give life to the entire tree and inspire new growth, so bishops and those in authority should judge their usefulness in terms of serving the clergy and congregations wherever they work. But it is not happening, for the reason given earlier: those in authority, by and large, have little experience of growth themselves. Basic to it all is not buildings, because buildings will crumble if faith dies, but people with a living and joyful faith.

I want to conclude my story with my unshakable conviction in the power of the Christian message with its corollary that our world needs it more than ever. There is no need to retreat into pessimism and faithlessness. The Church must change if it wishes to be a source of faith and blessing to the nation. It must recover its joy once more and perhaps rediscover gratitude for the privilege of being followers of the incomparable Jesus Christ. If leadership has become uncertain in recent years – and this is my reluctant conclusion – "wokeness" must be left behind. There must be a fresh determination to lead with energy, focus and faith. We must re-inhabit the message that created the church so many years ago and live it with a real sense of purpose and drive. And this takes me to the buildings that we have inherited from the past, not albatrosses around our necks to weigh us down or white elephants to wear us out with constant upkeep but spaces for service and worship. The moment they become impossible burdens we must not hesitate to reconsider their part in our mission. However, they are gifts from faithful generations from the past and many of them will continue to be sacred spaces for worship and renewal of life.

Ultimately, we should remind ourselves of our overweening tendency to a baseless hubris; even the Church is relatively unimportant because we exist only to serve the Kingdom of God. So Jesus said to his fearful disciples: "Do not be afraid, little flock, for your Father has been pleased to give you the kingdom." (Luke 12:32) It is not every business or organisation that can carry on its work knowing that victory is assured. But that is the promise and our Lord always keeps his word.

In November 2020 a dear American friend passed away, aged 90. His name was Bishop William Frey. Bill was a wonderful, outgoing man with a rich deep voice and a fund of stories. Among his "bon mots" one stands out. He said: "Hope is hearing the music of the future; faith is dancing to it today."

Notes

1   Paul Tillich, *The Shaking of the Foundations* (New York: Charles Scribner's Sons, 1955).

2   George Salmon, *The Infallibility of the Church* (London: John Murray, 1888).

3   Gregory the Great [c. AD 578-595], *Commentary on Job* (Collegeville, MN: Liturgical Press, 2015).

4   George L. Carey, *I Believe in Man* (London: Hodder and Stoughton, 1977).

5   John V. Taylor, *The Go-Between God* (London: SCM Press, 1972).

6   George L. Carey, *The Church in the Market Place* (Brighton: Kingsway Publications, 1989).

7   Gerald O'Collins, *Fundamental Theology* (New York: Paulist, 1981).

8   David Sheppard, *Bias to the Poor* (London: Hodder & Stoughton, 1983).

9   David Hirsch, "Jew hate and today's Left" in *The Jewish Chronicle*, 17 March 2016.

10   Jonathan Arkush: interview with Scott Simon, NPR Press, 31 March 2018.

11   T.E. Hulme, *Speculations: Essays on Humanism and the Philosophy of Art* (Abingdon: Routledge, 1960 [first published 1936]).

12   R.G. Collingwood, *Speculum Mentis* (Oxford: Oxford University Press, 1924).

13   James D. Wolfensohn, *A Global Life* (New York, NY: Public Affairs, 2010).

14   Wolfensohn, *Global Life*, p.288.

15   Robert Verkaik, *Posh Boys: How English Public Schools Ruin Britain* (London: Oneworld Publications, 2018).

16   Paul Badham, *Is There a Christian Case for Assisted Dying? Voluntary Euthanasia Reassessed* (London: SPCK, 2009), p.68.

17   Glanville Williams, *The Sanctity of Life and the Criminal Law* (New York NY: Alfred A Knopf, 1957).

18   Andrew Chandler, *George Bell, Bishop of Chichester: Church, State and Resistance in the Age of Dictatorship* (London: SPCK, 2016).

19   European Space Agency, "How many stars are there in the Universe?" https://www.esa.int/Science_Exploration/Space_Science/Herschel/How_many_stars_are_there_in_the_Universe [accessed 12 July 2021].

20   John Habgood, *Making Sense* (London: SPCK, 1993), p.53.

21   Saul Bellow, *Herzog* (New York: Viking Press, 1964).

22   Immanuel Kant, *Critik der reinen Vernunft* (German) (Riga: J.F. Hartknoch, 1781), published in English as *Critique of Pure Reason* (London: Penguin Classics, 2007).

23   Elie Wiesel, *Un di Velt Hot Geshvign* (Yiddish) (Buenos Aires: Central Union of Polish Jews in Argentina, 1956), published in English as *Night* (New York: Hill & Wang; London: MacGibbon & Kee, 1960).

24   Hans Urs von Balthasar, *The Glory of the Lord: A Theological Aesthetics* Vol 1: *Seeing the Form* (Edinburgh: T. & T. Clarke, 1983), p.69.

25   Larry Siedentop, *Inventing the Individual: The Origins of Western Liberalism* (London: Penguin, 2015).

26   Tom Holland, *Dominion: The Making of the Western Mind* (London: Little, Brown Book Group, 2019), p.219.

27   Holland, *Dominion*, p.524.

28   Peter Brown, *Through the Eye of a Needle: Wealth, the Fall of Rome and the Making of Christianity in the West, 350-550 AD* (Princeton, NJ: Princeton University Press, 2012). Similarly, see Peter Brown, *The Rise of Western Christendom: Triumph and Diversity, A.D. 200-1000* (Oxford: Blackwell, 1996), p.272f, on the civilising impact of Christianity.

Index